# PacketFence 7 Administration Guidemus

A catalogue record for this book is available from the Hong Kong Public Libraries.

Published in Hong Kong by Samurai Media Limited.

Email: info@samuraimedia.org

ISBN 978-988-8407-18-7



Background Cover Image by https://www.flickr.com/people/webtreatsetc/

# Table of Contents

# About this Guide

This guide will walk you through the installation and the day to day administration of the PacketFence solution.

The latest version of this guide is available at https://packetfence.org/documentation/

## Other sources of information

The following documents are included in the package and release tarballs.

| | |
|---|---|
| *Network Devices Configuration Guide* (pdf) | Covers switch, controllers and access points configuration. |
| *Developer's Guide* (pdf) | Covers captive portal customization, VLAN management customization and instructions for supporting new hardware. |
| `CREDITS` | This is, at least, a partial file of PacketFence contributors. |
| `NEWS.asciidoc` | Covers noteworthy features, improvements and bug fixes by release. |
| `UPGRADE.asciidoc` | Covers compatibility related changes, manual instructions and general notes about upgrading. |
| `ChangeLog` | Covers all changes to the source code. |

# Introduction

PacketFence is a fully supported, trusted, Free and Open Source network access control (NAC) system. Boosting an impressive feature set including a captive portal for registration and remediation, centralized wired and wireless management, 802.1X support, layer-2 isolation of problematic devices, integration with IDS, vulnerability scanners and firewalls; PacketFence can be used to effectively secure networks - from small to very large heterogeneous networks.

## Features

Out of band (VLAN Enforcement)
: PacketFence's operation is completely out of band when using VLAN enforcement which allows the solution to scale geographically and to be more resilient to failures.

In Band (Inline Enforcement)
: PacketFence can also be configured to be in-band, especially when you have non-manageable network switches or access points. PacketFence can also work with both VLAN and Inline enforcement activated for maximum scalability and security while allowing older hardware to still be secured using inline enforcement. Both layer-2 and layer-3 are supported for inline enforcement.

Hybrid support (Inline Enforcement with RADIUS support)
: PacketFence can also be configured as hybrid, if you have a manageable device that supports 802.1X and/or MAC-authentication. This feature can be enabled using a RADIUS attribute (MAC address, SSID, port) or using full inline mode on the equipment.

Hotspot support (Web Auth Enforcement)
: PacketFence can also be configured as hotspot, if you have a manageable device that supports an external captive portal (like Cisco WLC or Aruba IAP).

Voice over IP (VoIP) support
: Also called IP Telephony (IPT), VoIP is fully supported (even in heterogeneous environments) for multiple switch vendors (Cisco, Avaya, HP and many more).

802.1X
: 802.1X wireless and wired is supported through our FreeRADIUS module.

Wireless integration
: PacketFence integrates perfectly with wireless networks through our FreeRADIUS module. This allows you to secure your wired and wireless networks the same way using the same

user database and using the same captive portal, providing a consistent user experience. Mixing Access Points (AP) vendors and Wireless Controllers is supported.

| | |
|---|---|
| Registration | PacketFence supports an optional registration mechanism similar to "captive portal" solutions. Contrary to most captive portal solutions, PacketFence remembers users who previously registered and will automatically give them access without another authentication. Of course, this is configurable. An Acceptable Use Policy can be specified such that users cannot enable network access without first accepting it. |
| Detection of abnormal network activities | Abnormal network activities (computer virus, worms, spyware, traffic denied by establishment policy, etc.) can be detected using local and remote Snort or Suricata sensors. Beyond simple detection, PacketFence layers its own alerting and suppression mechanism on each alert type. A set of configurable actions for each violation is available to administrators. |
| Proactive vulnerability scans | Either Nessus , OpenVAS or WMI vulnerability scans can be performed upon registration, scheduled or on an ad-hoc basis. PacketFence correlates the scan engine vulnerability ID's of each scan to the violation configuration, returning content specific web pages about which vulnerability the host may have. |
| Isolation of problematic devices | PacketFence supports several isolation techniques, including VLAN isolation with VoIP support (even in heterogeneous environments) for multiple switch vendors. |
| Remediation through a captive portal | Once trapped, all network traffic is terminated by the PacketFence system. Based on the node's current status (unregistered, open violation, etc), the user is redirected to the appropriate URL. In the case of a violation, the user will be presented with instructions for the particular situation he/she is in reducing costly help desk intervention. |
| Firewall integration | PacketFence provides Single-Sign On features with many firewalls. Upon connection on the wired or wireless network, PacketFence can dynamically update the IP/user association on firewalls for them to apply, if required, per-user or per-group filtering policies. |
| Command-line and Web-based management | Web-based and command-line interfaces for all management tasks. |
| Guest Access | PacketFence supports a special guest VLAN out of the box. You configure your network so that the guest VLAN only goes out to the Internet and the registration VLAN and the captive portal are the components used to explain to the guest how to register for access and how his access works. This is usually branded by the organization offering the access. Several means of registering guests are possible. PacketFence does also support guest access bulk creations and imports. |

| | |
|---|---|
| Devices registration | A registered user can access a special Web page to register a device of his own. This registration process will require login from the user and then will register devices with pre-approved MAC OUI into a configurable category. |

PacketFence is developed by a community of developers located mainly in North America. More information can be found at https://packetfence.org.

# Network Integration

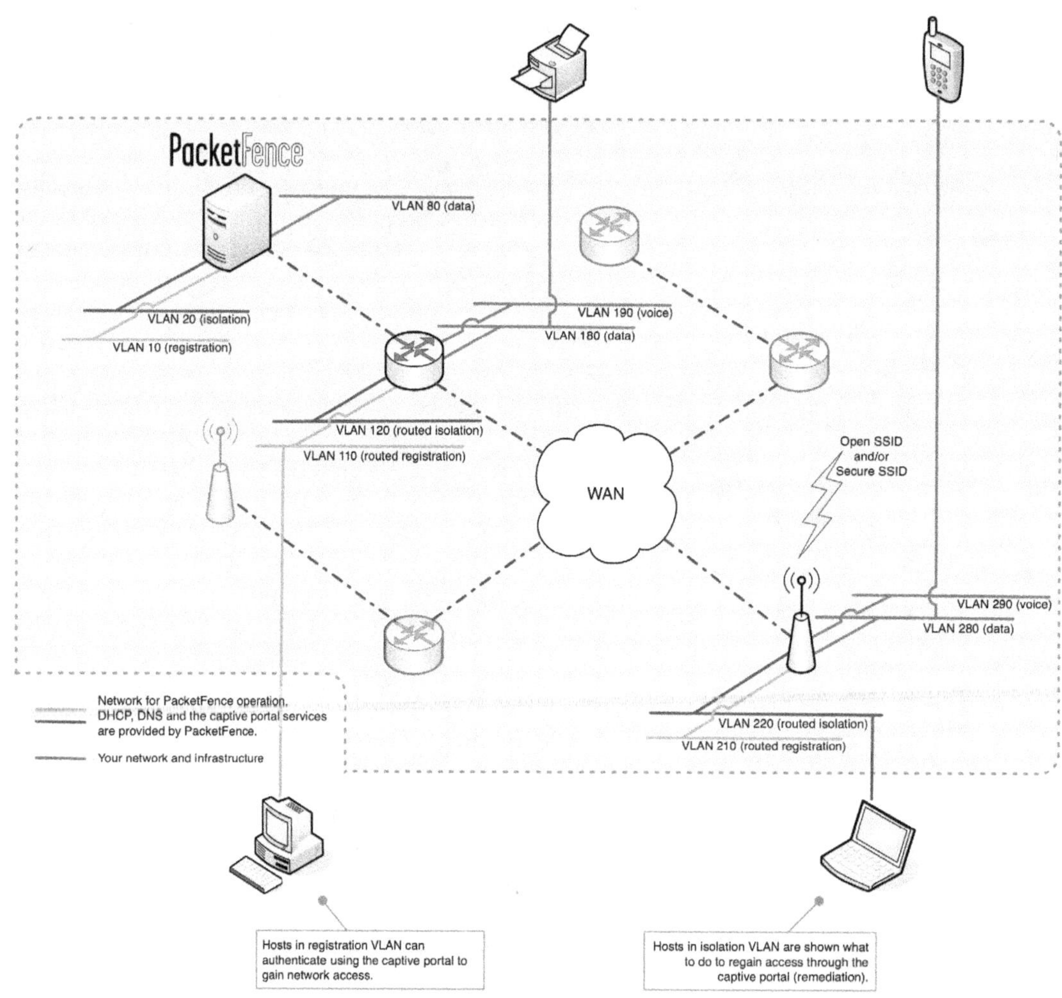


VLAN enforcement is pictured in the above diagram. Inline enforcement should be seen as a simple flat network where PacketFence acts as a firewall / gateway.

# Components

PacketFence requires various components to work such as a Web server, a database server, and a RADIUS server. It interacts with external tools to extend its functionalities.

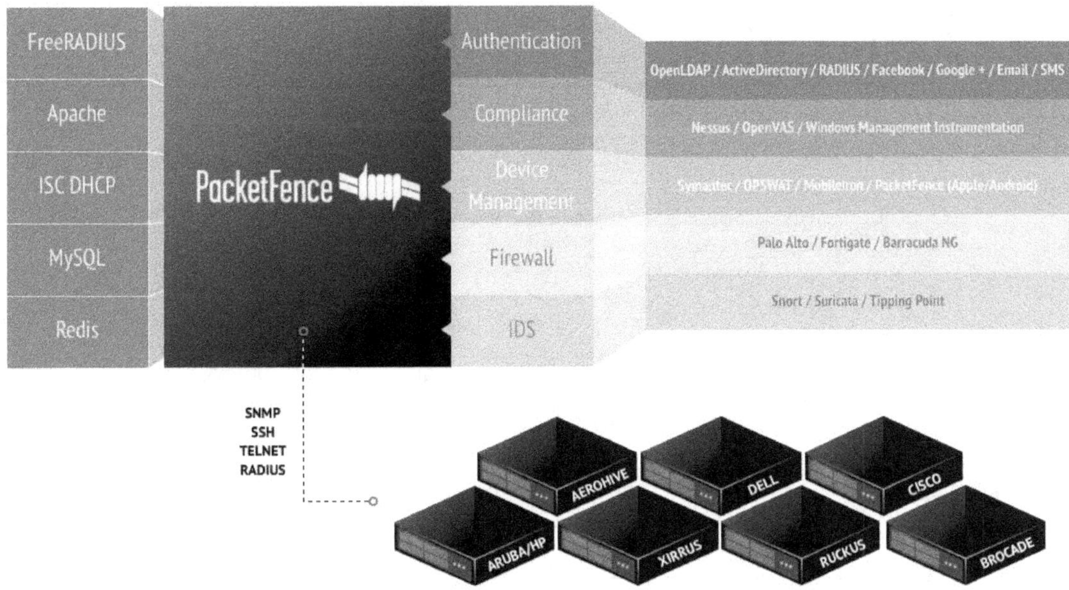

# System Requirements

## Assumptions

PacketFence reuses many components in an infrastructure. Thus, it requires the following ones:

- Database server (MySQL or MariaDB)
- Web server (Apache)
- DHCP server (ISC DHCP)
- RADIUS server (FreeRADIUS)

Depending on your setup you may have to install additional components like:

- NIDS (Snort/Suricata)

In this guide, we assume that all those components are running on the same server (i.e., "localhost" or "127.0.0.1") that PacketFence will be installed on.

Good understanding of those underlying component and GNU/Linux is required to install PacketFence. If you miss some of those required components, please refer to the appropriate documentation and proceed with the installation of these requirements before continuing with this guide.

## Minimum Hardware Requirements

The following provides a list of the minimum server hardware recommendations:

- Intel or AMD CPU 3 GHz
- 8 GB of RAM
- 100 GB of disk space (RAID-1 recommended)
- 1 Network card (2 recommended)

## Operating System Requirements

PacketFence supports the following operating systems on the x86_64 architectures:

 

- Red Hat Enterprise Linux 6.x and 7.x Server
- Community ENTerprise Operating System (CentOS) 6.x and 7.x
- Debian 7.0 (Wheezy) and 8.0 (Jessie)

Make sure that you can install additional packages from your standard distribution. For example, if you are using Red Hat Enterprise Linux, you have to be subscribed to the Red Hat Network before continuing with the PacketFence software installation.

Other distributions such as Fedora and Gentoo are known to work but this document doesn't cover them.

## Services start-up

PacketFence takes care of handling the operation of the following services:

- Web server (httpd)
- DHCP server (dhcpd)
- FreeRADIUS server (radiusd)
- Snort/Suricata Network IDS (snort/suricata)
- Firewall (iptables)

**Make sure that all the other services are automatically started by your operating system!**

# Installation

This section will guide you through the installation of PacketFence together with its dependencies.

## OS Installation

Install your distribution with minimal installation and no additional packages. Then:

- Disable Firewall
- Disable SELinux
- Disable AppArmor
- Disable resolvconf

Make sure your system is up to date and your yum or apt-get database is updated. On a RHEL-based system, do:

```
yum update
```

On a Debian or Ubuntu system, do:

```
apt-get update
apt-get upgrade
```

Regarding SELinux or AppArmor, even if these features may be wanted by some organizations, PacketFence will not run properly if SELinux or AppArmor are enabled. You will need to explicitly disable SELinux in the `/etc/selinux/config` file and AppArmor with **update-rc.d -f apparmor stop**, **update-rc.d -f apparmor teardown** and **update-rc.d -f apparmor remove**. Regarding resolvconf, you can remove the symlink to that file and simply create the `/etc/resolv.conf` file with the content you want.

### RedHat-based systems

Note

Applies to CentOS and Scientific Linux but only the x86_64 architecture is supported.

Explicitly instruct NetworkManager to never interact with your DNS configuration (Source):

```
echo "[main]
dns=none" > /etc/NetworkManager/conf.d/99-no-dns.conf
service NetworkManager restart
```

## RHEL 6.x

Note

These are extra steps are required for RHEL 6 systems only, excluding derivatives such as CentOS or Scientific Linux.

RedHat Enterprise Linux users need to take an additional setup step. If you are not using the RHN Subscription Management from RedHat you need to enable the optional channel by running the following as root:

```
subscription-manager repos --enable rhel-6-server-optional-rpms
```

## RHEL 7.x

Note

These are extra steps are required for RHEL 7 systems only, excluding derivatives such as CentOS or Scientific Linux.

RedHat Enterprise Linux users need to take an additional setup step. If you are not using the RHN Subscription Management from RedHat you need to enable the optional channel by running the following as root:

```
subscription-manager repos --enable rhel-7-server-optional-rpms
```

## Debian

All the PacketFence dependencies are available through the official repositories.

# Software Download

PacketFence provides a RPM repository for RHEL / CentOS instead of a single RPM file.

For Debian, PacketFence also provides package repositories.

These repositories contain all required dependencies to install PacketFence. This provides numerous advantages:

- easy installation
- everything is packaged as RPM/deb (no more CPAN hassle)
- easy upgrade

# Software Installation

## RHEL / CentOS

In order to use the PacketFence repository :

```
# yum localinstall http://packetfence.org/downloads/PacketFence/RHEL7/`uname -i`/
RPMS/packetfence-release-1.2-6.el7.centos.noarch.rpm
```

Once the repository is defined, you can install PacketFence with all its dependencies, and the required external services (Database server, DHCP server, RADIUS server) using:

```
yum install perl
yum install --enablerepo=packetfence packetfence
```

Once installed, the Web-based configuration interface will automatically be started. You can access it from https://@ip_of_packetfence:1443/configurator

## Debian

For Debian 7:

In order to use the repository, create a file named `/etc/apt/sources.list.d/packetfence.list`:

```
echo 'deb http://inverse.ca/downloads/PacketFence/debian wheezy wheezy' > /etc/
apt/sources.list.d/packetfence.list
```

For Debian 8:

In order to use the repository, create a file named `/etc/apt/sources.list.d/packetfence.list`:

```
echo 'deb http://inverse.ca/downloads/PacketFence/debian jessie jessie' > /etc/
apt/sources.list.d/packetfence.list
```

Once the repository is defined, you can install PacketFence with all its dependencies, and the required external services (Database server, DHCP server, RADIUS server) using:

```
sudo apt-key adv --keyserver keys.gnupg.net --recv-key 0x810273C4
sudo apt-get update
sudo apt-get install packetfence
```

# Get off on the right foot

Prior configuring PacketFence, you must chose an appropriate enforcement mode to be used by PacketFence with your networking equipment. The enforcement mode is the technique used to enforce registration and any subsequent access of devices on your network. PacketFence supports the following enforcement modes:

- Inline
- Out-of-band
- Hybrid

It is also possible to combine enforcement modes. For example, you could use the out-of-band mode on your wired switches, while using the inline mode on your old WiFi access points.

The following sections will explain these enforcement modes. If you decide to use the inline mode, please refer to the PacketFence Inline Deployment Quick Guide using ZEN for a complete configuration example. If you decide to use the out-of-band mode, please refer to the PacketFence Out-of-Band Deployment Quick Guide using ZEN

# Technical introduction to Inline enforcement

## Introduction

Before the version 3.0 of PacketFence, it was not possible to support unmanageable devices such as entry-level consumer switches or access-points. Now, with the new inline mode, PacketFence can be use in-band for those devices. So in other words, PacketFence would become the gateway of that inline network, and NAT or route the traffic using IPTables/IPSet to the Internet (or to another section of the network). Let see how it works.

## Device configuration

No special configuration is needed on the unmanageable device. That's the beauty of it. You only need to ensure that the device is "talking" on the inline VLAN. At this point, all the traffic will be passing through PacketFence since it is the gateway for this VLAN.

## Access control

The access control relies entirely on IPTables/IPSet. When a user is not registered, and connects in the inline VLAN, PacketFence will give him an IP address. At this point, the user will be marked as unregistered in the ipset session, and all the Web traffic will be redirected to the captive portal and other traffic blocked. The user will have to register through the captive portal as in VLAN enforcement. When he registers, PacketFence changes the device´s ipset session to allow the user's mac address to go through it.

# Limitations

Inline enforcement because of it's nature has several limitations that one must be aware of.

- Everyone behind an inline interface is on the same Layer 2 LAN
- Every packet of authorized users goes through the PacketFence server increasing the server's load considerably: Plan ahead for capacity
- Every packet of authorized users goes through the PacketFence server: it is a single point of failure for Internet access
- Ipset can store up to 65536 entries, so it is not possible to have a inline network class upper than B

This is why it is considered a poor man's way of doing access control. We have avoided it for a long time because of the above mentioned limitations. That said, being able to perform both inline and VLAN enforcement on the same server at the same time is a real advantage: it allows users to maintain maximum security while they deploy new and more capable network hardware providing a clean migration path to VLAN enforcement.

# Technical introduction to Out-of-band enforcement

## Introduction

VLAN assignment is currently performed using several different techniques. These techniques are compatible one to another but not on the same switch port. This means that you can use the more secure and modern techniques for your latest switches and another technique on the old switches that doesn't support latest techniques. As it's name implies, VLAN assignment means that PacketFence is the server that assigns the VLAN to a device. This VLAN can be one of your VLANs or it can be a special VLAN where PacketFence presents the captive portal for authentication or remediation.

VLAN assignment effectively isolate your hosts at the OSI Layer2 meaning that it is the trickiest method to bypass and is the one which adapts best to your environment since it glues into your current VLAN assignment methodology.

## VLAN assignment techniques

### Wired: 802.1X + MAC Authentication

802.1X provides port-based authentication, which involves communications between a supplicant, authenticator (known as NAS), and authentication server (known as AAA). The supplicant is often software on a client device, such as a laptop, the authenticator is a wired Ethernet switch or wireless access point, and the authentication server is generally a RADIUS server.

The supplicant (i.e., client device) is not allowed access through the authenticator to the network until the supplicant's identity is authorized. With 802.1X port-based authentication, the supplicant provides credentials, such as user name / password or digital certificate, to the authenticator, and the authenticator forwards the credentials to the authentication server for verification. If the credentials are valid (in the authentication server database), the supplicant (client device) is allowed to access the network. The protocol for authentication is called Extensible Authentication Protocol (EAP) which have many variants. Both supplicant and authentication servers need to speak the same EAP protocol. Most popular EAP variant is PEAP-MsCHAPv2 (supported by Windows / Mac OSX / Linux for authentication against AD).

In this context, PacketFence runs the authentication server (a FreeRADIUS instance) and will return the appropriate VLAN to the switch. A module that integrates in FreeRADIUS does a remote call to the PacketFence server to obtain that information. More and more devices have 802.1X supplicant which makes this approach more and more popular.

MAC Authentication is a new mechanism introduced by some switch vendor to handle the cases where a 802.1X supplicant does not exist. Different vendors have different names for it. Cisco calls it MAC Authentication Bypass (MAB), Juniper calls it MAC RADIUS, Extreme Networks calls it Netlogin, etc. After a timeout period, the switch will stop trying to perform 802.1X and will fallback to MAC Authentication. It has the advantage of using the same approach as 802.1X except that the MAC address is sent instead of the user name and there is no end-to-end EAP conversation (no strong authentication). Using MAC Authentication, devices like network printer or non-802.1X capable IP Phones can still gain access to the network and the right VLAN.

## Wireless: 802.1X + MAC authentication

Wireless 802.1X works like wired 802.1X and MAC authentication is the same as wired MAC Authentication. Where things change is that the 802.1X is used to setup the security keys for encrypted communication (WPA2-Enterprise) while MAC authentication is only used to authorize (allow or disallow) a MAC on the wireless network.

On wireless networks, the usual PacketFence setup dictate that you configure two SSIDs: an open one and a secure one. The open one is used to help users configure the secure one properly and requires authentication over the captive portal (which runs in HTTPS).

The following diagram demonstrates the flow between a mobile endpoint, a WiFi access point, a WiFi controller and PacketFence:

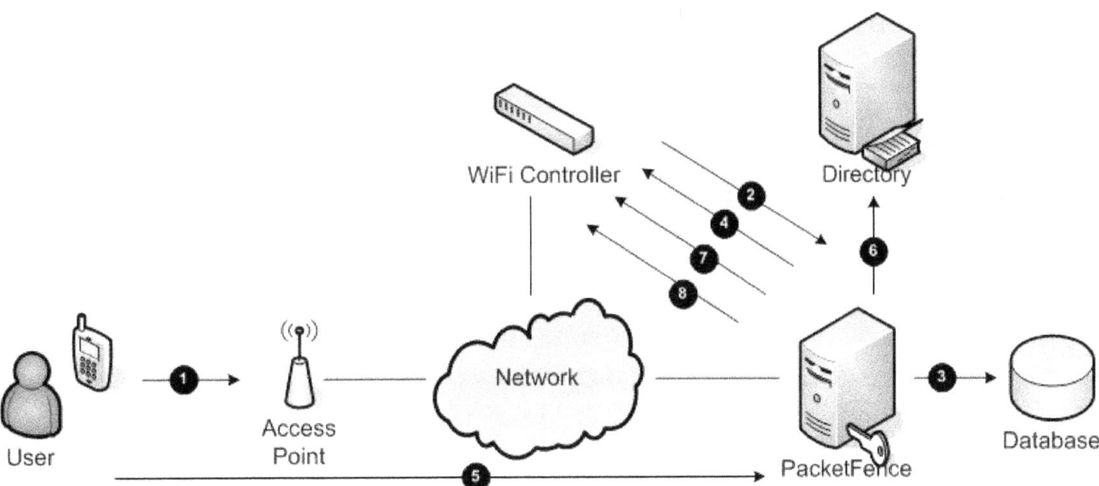


1. User initiates association to WLAN AP and transmits MAC address. If user accesses network via a registered device in PacketFence go to 8
2. The WLAN controller transmits MAC address via RADIUS to the PacketFence server to authenticate/authorize that MAC address on the AP
3. PacketFence server conducts address audit in its database. If it does not recognize the MAC address go to 4. If it does go to 8.
4. PacketFence server directs WLAN controller via RADIUS (RFC2868 attributes) to put the device in an "unauthenticated role" (set of ACLs that would limit/redirect the user to the PacketFence

captive portal for registration, or we can also use a registration VLAN in which PacketFence does DNS blackholing and is the DHCP server)

5. The user's device issues a DHCP/DNS request to PacketFence (which is a DHCP/DNS server on this VLAN or for this role) which sends the IP and DNS information. At this point, ACLs are limiting/redirecting the user to the PacketFence's captive portal for authentication. PacketFence fingerprints the device (user-agent attributes, DHCP information & MAC address patterns) to which it can take various actions including: keep device on registration portal, direct to alternate captive portal, auto-register the device, auto-block the device, etc. If the device remains on the registration portal the user registers by providing the information (username/password, cell phone number, etc.). At this time PacketFence could also require the device to go through a posture assessment (using Nessus, OpenVAS, etc.)
6. If authentication is required (username/password) through a login form, those credentials are validated via the Directory server (or any other authentication sources - like LDAP, SQL, RADIUS, SMS, Facebook, Google+, etc.) which provides user attributes to PacketFence which creates user +device policy profile in its database.
7. PacketFence performs a Change of Authorization (RFC3576) on the controller and the user must be re-authenticated/reauthorized, so we go back to 1
8. PacketFence server directs WLAN controller via RADIUS to put the device in an "authenticated role", or in the "normal" VLAN

## Web Auth mode

Web authentication is a method on the switch that forwards HTTP traffic of the device to the captive portal. With this mode, your device will never change of VLAN ID but only the ACL associated to your device will change. Refer to the Network Devices Configuration Guide to see a sample web auth configuration on a Cisco WLC.

## Port-security and SNMP

Relies on the port-security SNMP Traps. A fake static MAC address is assigned to all the ports this way any MAC address will generate a security violation and a trap will be sent to PacketFence. The system will authorize the MAC and set the port in the right VLAN. VoIP support is possible but tricky. It varies a lot depending on the switch vendor. Cisco is well supported but isolation of a PC behind an IP Phone leads to an interesting dilemma: either you shut the port (and the phone at the same time) or you change the data VLAN but the PC doesn't do DHCP (didn't detect link was down) so it cannot reach the captive portal.

Aside from the VoIP isolation dilemma, it is the technique that has proven to be reliable and that has the most switch vendor support.

# More on SNMP traps VLAN isolation

When the VLAN isolation is working through SNMP traps all switch ports (on which VLAN isolation should be done) must be configured to send SNMP traps to the PacketFence host. On PacketFence, we use snmptrapd as the SNMP trap receiver. As it receives traps, it reformats and writes them into a flat file: `/usr/local/pf/logs/snmptrapd.log`. The multithreaded `pfsetvlan` daemon reads these traps from the flat file and responds to them by setting the switch port to the correct VLAN. Currently, we support switches from Cisco, Edge-core, HP, Intel, Linksys and Nortel (adding support for switches from another vendor implies extending the `pf::Switch` class). Depending on your switches capabilities, `pfsetvlan` will act on different types of SNMP traps.

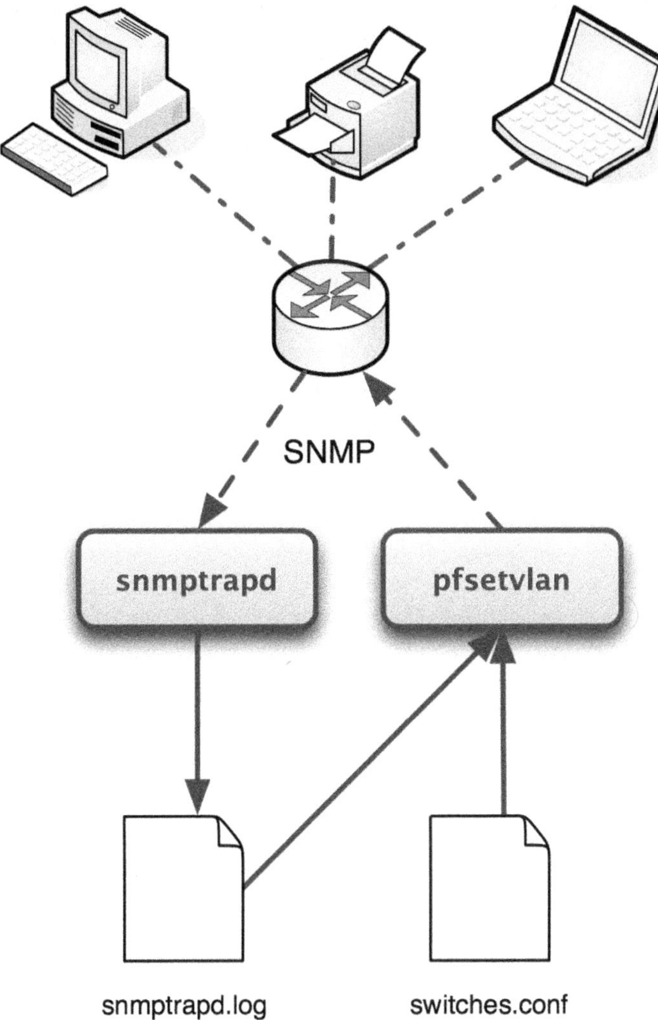


You need to create a registration VLAN (with a DHCP server, but no routing to other VLANs) in which PacketFence will put unregistered devices. If you want to isolate computers which have open violations in a separate VLAN, an isolation VLAN needs also to be created.

## linkUp/linkDown traps (deprecated)

This is the most basic setup and it needs a third VLAN: the MAC detection VLAN. There should be nothing in this VLAN (no DHCP server) and it should not be routed anywhere; it is just an void VLAN.

When a host connects to a switch port, the switch sends a linkUp trap to PacketFence. Since it takes some time before the switch learns the MAC address of the newly connected device, PacketFence immediately puts the port in the MAC detection VLAN in which the device will send DHCP requests (with no answer) in order for the switch to learn its MAC address. Then pfsetvlan will send periodical

SNMP queries to the switch until the switch learns the MAC of the device. When the MAC address is known, pfsetvlan checks its status (existing ? registered ? any violations ?) in the database and puts the port in the appropriate VLAN. When a device is unplugged, the switch sends a *linkDown* trap to PacketFence which puts the port into the MAC detection VLAN.

When a computer boots, the initialization of the NIC generates several link status changes. And every time the switch sends a linkUp and a linkDown trap to PacketFence. Since PacketFence has to act on each of these traps, this generates unfortunately some unnecessary load on pfsetvlan. In order to optimize the trap treatment, PacketFence stops every thread for a *linkUp trap* when it receives a *linkDown* trap on the same port. But using only linkUp/linkDown traps is not the most scalable option. For example in case of power failure, if hundreds of computers boot at the same time, PacketFence would receive a lot of traps almost instantly and this could result in network connection latency.

## MAC notification traps

If your switches support MAC notification traps (MAC learnt, MAC removed), we suggest that you activate them in addition to the linkUp/linkDown traps. This way, pfsetvlan does not need, after a linkUp trap, to query the switch continuously until the MAC has finally been learned. When it receives a linkUp trap for a port on which MAC notification traps are also enabled, it only needs to put the port in the MAC detection VLAN and can then free the thread. When the switch learns the MAC address of the device it sends a MAC learnt trap (containing the MAC address) to PacketFence.

## Port Security traps

In its most basic form, the Port Security feature remembers the MAC address connected to the switch port and allows only that MAC address to communicate on that port. If any other MAC address tries to communicate through the port, port security will not allow it and send a port-security trap.

If your switches support this feature, **we strongly recommend to use it rather than linkUp/linkDown and/or MAC notifications**. Why? Because as long as a MAC address is authorized on a port and is the only one connected, the switch will send no trap whether the device reboots, plugs in or unplugs. This drastically reduces the SNMP interactions between the switches and PacketFence.

When you enable port security traps you should not enable linkUp/linkDown nor MAC notification traps.

# Technical introduction to Hybrid enforcement

## Introduction

In previous versions of PacketFence, it was not possible to have RADIUS enabled for inline enforcement mode. Now with the new hybrid mode, all the devices that supports 802.1X or MAC-authentication can work with this mode. Let's see how it works.

## Device configuration

You need to configure inline enforcement mode in PacketFence and configure your switch(es) / access point(s) to use the VLAN assignment techniques (802.1X or MAC-authentication). You also need to take care of a specific parameter in the switch configuration window, "Trigger to enable inline mode". This parameter is working like a trigger and you have the possibility to define different sort of triggers:

ALWAYS , PORT , MAC , SSID
: where ALWAYS means that the device is always in inline mode, PORT specify the ifIndex of the port which will use inline enforcement, MAC a mac address that will be put in inline enforcement technique rather than VLAN enforcement and SSID an ssid name. An example:

```
SSID::GuestAccess,MAC::00:11:22:33:44:55
```

This will trigger all the nodes that connects to the *GuestAccess* SSID to use inline enforcement mode (PacketFence will return a void VLAN or the `inlineVlan` if defined in switch configuration) and the MAC address `00:11:22:33:44:55` client if it connects on another SSID.

# Configuration

At this point in the documentation, PacketFence should be installed. You would also have chosen the right enforcement method for you and completed the initial configuration of PacketFence. The following section presents key concepts and features in PacketFence.

PacketFence provides a web-based administration interface for easy configuration and operational management. If you went through PacketFence's web-based configuration tool, you should have set the password for the `admin` user.

Once PacketFence is started, the administration interface is available at: https://@ip_of_packetfence:1443/

The next key steps are important to understand how PacketFence works. In order to get the solution working, you must first understand and configure the following aspects of the solution in this specific order:

1. **roles** - a role in PacketFence will be eventually be mapped to a VLAN, an ACL or an external role. You must define the roles to use in your organization for network access
2. **authentication** - once roles are defined, you must create an appropriate authentication source in PacketFence. That will allow PacketFence to compute the right role to be used for an endpoint, or the user using it
3. **network devices** - once your roles and authentication sources are defined, you must add switches, WiFi controllers or APs to be managed by PacketFence. When doing so, you will configure how roles are being mapped to VLAN, ACLs or external roles
4. **connection profiles** - at this point, you are almost ready to test. You will need to set which authentication sources are to be used on the default captive portal, or create an other one to suit your needs
5. test!

Note

If you plan to use 802.1X - please see the *FreeRADIUS Configuration* section below.

## Roles Management

Roles in PacketFence can be created from PacketFence administrative GUI - from the **Configuration → Policies and Access Control → Roles** section. From this interface, you can also limit the number of devices users belonging to certain roles can register.

Roles are dynamically computed by PacketFence, based on the rules (ie., a set of conditions and actions) from authentication sources, using a first-match wins algorithm. Roles are then matched to VLAN or internal roles or ACL on equipment from the **Configuration → Policies and Access Control → Switches** module.

# Authentication

PacketFence can authenticate users that register devices via the captive portal using various methods. Among the supported methods, there are:

- Active Directory
- Apache htpasswd file
- Email
- External HTTP API
- Facebook (OAuth 2)
- Github (OAuth 2)
- Google (OAuth 2)
- Instagram (OAuth 2)
- Kerberos
- Kickbox
- LDAP
- LinkedIn (OAuth 2)
- Null
- Pinterest (OAuth 2)
- RADIUS
- SMS
- Sponsored Email
- Twitter (OAuth 2)
- Windows Live (OAuth 2)

Moreover, PacketFence can also authenticate users defined in its own internal SQL database. Authentication sources can be created from PacketFence administrative GUI - from the **Configuration → Policies and Access Control → Sources** section. Alternatively (but not recommended), authentication sources, rules, conditions and actions can be configured from `conf/authentication.conf`.

Each authentication sources you define will have a set of rules, conditions and actions.

Multiple authentication sources can be defined, and will be tested in the order specified (note that they can be reordered from the GUI by dragging them around). Each source can have multiple rules, which will also be tested in the order specified. Rules can also be reordered, just like sources. Finally, conditions can be defined for a rule to match certain criteria. If the criteria match (one or more), action are then applied and rules testing stop, across all sources as this is a "first match wins" operation.

When no condition is defined, the rule will be considered as a catch-all. When a catch-all is defined, all actions will be applied for any users that match in the authentication source.

Once a source is defined, it can be used from **Configuration → Policies and Access Control → Connection Profiles**. Each connection profile has a list of authentication sources to use.

## Example

Let's say we have two roles: guest and employee. First, we define them **Configuration → Policies and Access Control → Roles**.

Now, we want to authenticate employees using Active Directory (over LDAP), and guests using PacketFence's internal database - both using PacketFence's captive portal. From the **Configuration → Policies and Access Control → Sources**, we select **Add source → AD**. We provide the following information:

- **Name:** ad1
- **Description:** Active Directory for Employees
- **Host:** 192.168.1.2:389 without SSL/TLS
- **Base DN:** CN=Users,DC=acme,DC=local
- **Scope:** One-level
- **Username Attribute:** sAMAccountName
- **Bind DN:** CN=Administrator,CN=Users,DC=acme,DC=local
- **Password:** acme123

Then, we add a rule by clicking on the **Add rule** button and provide the following information:

- **Name:** employees
- **Description:** Rule for all employees
- Don't set any condition (as it's a catch-all rule)
- Set the following **actions:**

  - Set role employee

  - Set unregistration date January 1st, 2020

Test the connection and save everything. Using the newly defined source, any username that actually matches in the source (using the sAMAccountName) will have the employee role and an unregistration date set to January 1st, 2020.

Now, since we want to authenticate guests from PacketFence's internal SQL database, accounts must be provisioned manually. You can do so from the **Users → Create** section. When creating guests, specify "guest" for the **Set role** action, and set an access duration for 1 day.

If you would like to differentiate user authentication and machine authentication using Active Directory, one way to do it is by creating a second authentication sources, for machines:

- **Name:** ad1

- **Description:** Active Directory for Machines
- **Host:** 192.168.1.2:389 without SSL/TLS
- **Base DN:** CN=Computers,DC=acme,DC=local
- **Scope:** One-level
- **Username Attribute:** servicePrincipalName
- **Bind DN:** CN=Administrator,CN=Users,DC=acme,DC=local
- **Password:** acme123

Then, we add a rule:

- Name:* machines
- **Description:** Rule for all machines
- Don't set any condition (as it's a catch-all rule)
- Set the following **actions:**
    - Set role machineauth
    - Set unregistration date January 1st, 2020

Note

When a rule is defined as a catch-all, it will always match if the username attribute matches the queried one. This applies for Active Directory, LDAP and Apache htpasswd file sources. Kerberos and RADIUS will act as true catch-all, and accept everything.

Note

If you want to use other LDAP attributes in your authentication source, add them in *Configuration→System Configuration→Main Configuration→Advanced→Custom LDAP attributes*. They will then be available in the rules you define.

# External API authentication

PacketFence also supports calling an external HTTP API as an authentication source. The external API needs to implement an authentication action and an authorization action.

## Authentication

This should provide the information about whether or not the username/password combination is valid

These information are available through the POST fields of the request

The server should reply with two attributes in a JSON response

- **result** : should be 1 for success, 0 for failure
- **message** : should be the reason it succeeded or failed

Example JSON response :

```
{"result":1,"message":"Valid username and password"}
```


## Authorization

This should provide the actions to apply on a user based on it's attributes

The following attributes are available for the reply : **access_duration**, **access_level**, **sponsor**, **unregdate**, **category**.

Sample JSON response, note that not all attributes are necessary, only send back what you need.


```
{"access_duration":"1D","access_level":"ALL","sponsor":1
  ,"unregdate":"2030-01-01","category":"default"}
```

### Note

See /usr/local/pf/addons/example_external_auth for an example implementation compatible with PacketFence.

## PacketFence configuration

In PacketFence, you need to configure an HTTP source in order to use an external API.

Here is a brief description of the fields :

- **Host** : First, the protocol, then the IP address or hostname of the API and lastly the port to connect to the API.
- **API username and password** : If your API implements HTTP basic authentication (RFC 2617) you can add them in these fields. Leaving any of those two fields empty will make PacketFence do the requests without any authentication.
- **Authentication URL** : URL relative to the host to call when doing the authentication of a user. Note that it is automatically prefixed by a slash.
- **Authorization URL** : URL relative to the host to call when doing the authorization of a user. Note that it is automatically prefixed by a slash.

# SAML authentication

PacketFence supports SAML authentication in the captive portal in combination with another internal source to define the level of authorization of the user.

First, transfer the Identity Provider metadata on the PacketFence server. In this example, it will be under the path `/usr/local/pf/conf/idp-metadata.xml`.

Then, transfer the certificate and CA certificate of the Identity provider on the server. In this example, they will be under the paths `/usr/local/pf/conf/ssl/idp.crt` and `/usr/local/pf/conf/ssl/idp-ca.crt`. If it is a self-signed certificate, then you will be able to use it as the CA in the PacketFence configuration.

Then, to configure SAML in PacketFence, go in *Configuration → Policies and Access Control → Sources* and then create a new Internal source of the type SAML and configure it.

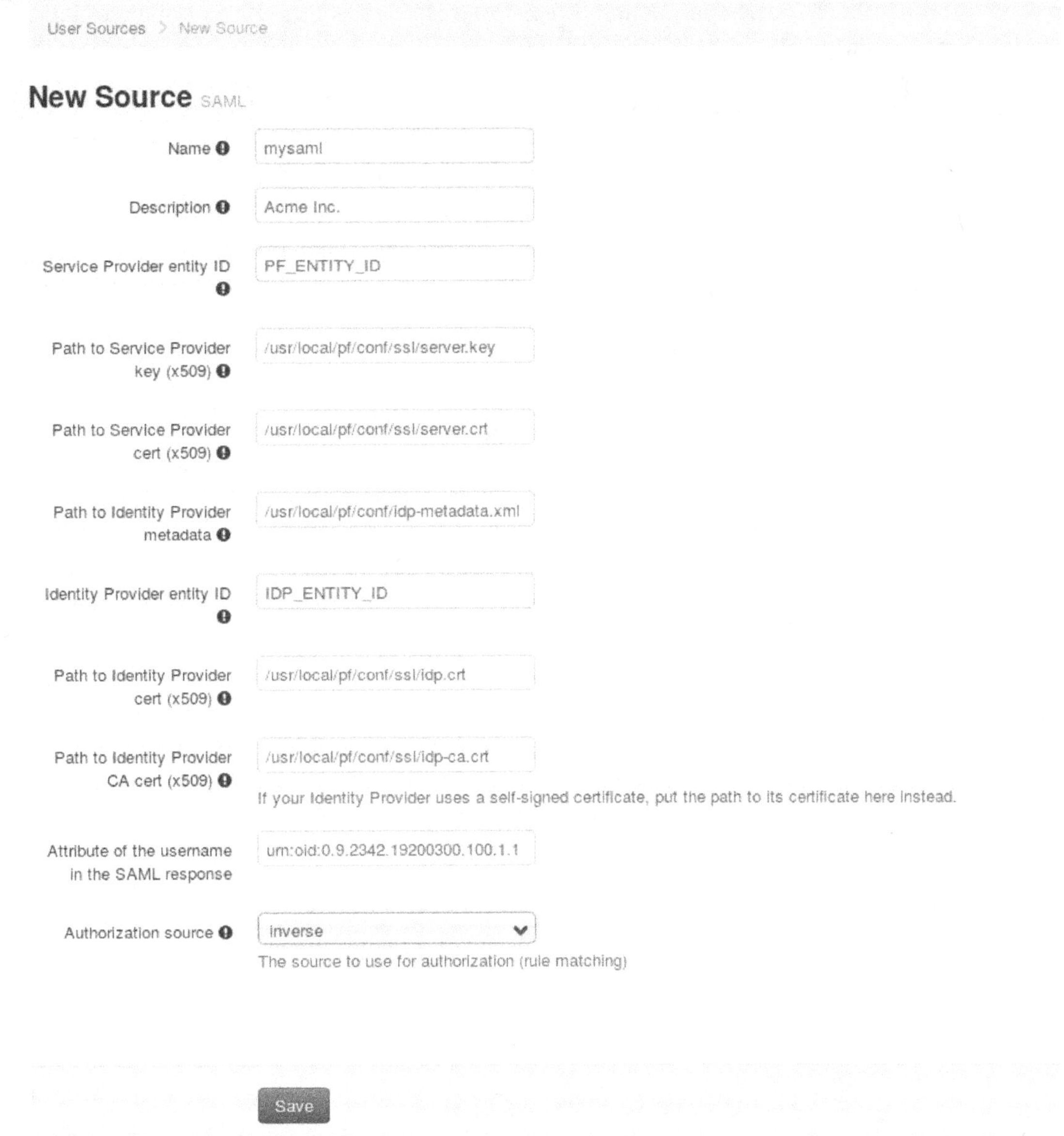


Where :

- **Service Provider entity ID** is the identifier of the Service Provider (PacketFence). Make sure this matches your Identity Provider configuration.
- **Path to Service Provider key** is the path to the key that will be used by PacketFence to sign its messages to the Identity Provider. A default one is provided under the path : `/usr/local/pf/conf/ssl/server.key`
- **Path to Service Provider cert** is the path to the certificate associated to the key above. A self-signed one is provided under the path : `/usr/local/pf/conf/ssl/server.key`
- **Path to Identity Provider metadata** is the path to the metadata file you transferred above (should be in `/usr/local/pf/conf/idp-metadata.xml`)
- **Path to Identity Provider cert** is the path to the certificate of the identity provider you transferred on the server above (should be in `/usr/local/pf/conf/ssl/idp.crt`).

- **Path to Identity Provider CA cert** is the path to the CA certificate of the identity provider you transferred on the server above (should be in `/usr/local/pf/conf/ssl/ca-idp.crt`). If the certificate above is self-signed, put the same path as above in this field.
- **Attribute of the username in the SAML response** is the attribute that contains the username in the SAML assertion returned by your Identity Provider. The default should fit at least SimpleSAMLphp.
- **Authorization source** is the source that will be used to match the username against the rules defined in it. This allows to set the role and access duration of the user. The *Authentication* section of this document contains explanations on how to configure an LDAP source which can then be used here.

Once this is done, save the source and you will be able to download the Service Provider metadata for PacketFence using the link *Download Service Provider metadata* on the page.

Configure your identity provider according to the generated metadata to complete the Trust between PacketFence and your Identity Provider.

In the case of SimpleSAMLPHP, the following configuration was used in `metadata/saml20-sp-remote.php` :

```
$metadata['PF_ENTITY_ID'] = array(
   'AssertionConsumerService' => 'http://PORTAL_HOSTNAME/saml/assertion',
   'SingleLogoutService' => 'http://PORTAL_HOSTNAME/saml/logoff',
);
```

Note

PacketFence does not support logoff on the SAML Identity Provider. You can still define the URL in the metadata but it will not be used.

## Passthroughs

In order for your users to be able to access the Identity Provider login page, you will need to activate passthroughs and add the Identity Provider domain to the allowed passthroughs.

To do so, go in *Configuration* → *Network Configuration* → *Networks* → *Fencing*, then check *Passthrough* and add the Identity Provider domain name to the *Passhtroughs* list.

Next, restart iptables and pfdns to apply your new passthroughs.

# Network Devices Definition (switches.conf)

This section applies only for VLAN enforcement. Users planning to do inline enforcement only can skip this section.

PacketFence needs to know which switches, access points or controllers it manages, their type and configuration. All this information is stored in `/usr/local/pf/conf/switches.conf`. You can modify the configuration directly in the `switches.conf` file or you can do it from the Web Administration panel under **Configuration → Policies and Access Control → Switches** - which is now the preferred way.

The `/usr/local/pf/conf/switches.conf` configuration file contains a default section including:

- Default SNMP read/write communities for the switches
- Default working mode (see the note below about possible working modes)

and a switch section for each switch (managed by PacketFence) including:

- Switch IP/Mac/Range
- Switch vendor/type
- Switch uplink ports (trunks and non-managed IfIndex)
- per-switch re-definition of the VLANs (if required)

Note

`switches.conf` is loaded at startup. A reload is required when changes are manually made to this file `/usr/local/pf/bin/pfcmd configreload`.

## Working modes

There are three different working modes for a switch in PacketFence:

Testing
: pfsetvlan writes in the log files what it would normally do, but it doesn't do anything.

Registration
: pfsetvlan automatically-register all MAC addresses seen on the switch ports. As in testing mode, no VLAN changes are done.

Production
: pfsetvlan sends the SNMP writes to change the VLAN on the switch ports.

## RADIUS

To set the RADIUS secret, set it from the Web administrative interface when adding a switch. Alternatively, edit the switch config file (`/usr/local/pf/conf/switches.conf`) and set the following parameters:

```
radiusSecret = secretPassPhrase
```

Moreover, the RADIUS secret is required to support the RADIUS Dynamic Authentication (Change of authorization or Disconnect) as defined in RFC3576.

## SNMP v1, v2c and v3

PacketFence uses SNMP to communicate with most switches. PacketFence also supports SNMP v3. You can use SNMP v3 for communication in both directions: from the switch to PacketFence and from PacketFence to the switch. SNMP usage is discouraged, you should now use RADIUS. However, even if RADIUS is being used, some switches might also require SNMP to be configured to work properly with PacketFence.

### From PacketFence to a switch

Edit the switch config file (`/usr/local/pf/conf/switches.conf`) and set the following parameters:

```
SNMPVersion = 3
SNMPUserNameRead = readUser
SNMPAuthProtocolRead = MD5
SNMPAuthPasswordRead = authpwdread
SNMPPrivProtocolRead = AES
SNMPPrivPasswordRead = privpwdread
SNMPUserNameWrite = writeUser
SNMPAuthProtocolWrite = MD5
SNMPAuthPasswordWrite = authpwdwrite
SNMPPrivProtocolWrite = AES
SNMPPrivPasswordWrite = privpwdwrite
```

### From a switch to PacketFence

Edit the switch config file (`/usr/local/pf/conf/switches.conf`) and set the following parameters:

```
SNMPVersionTrap = 3
SNMPUserNameTrap = readUser
SNMPAuthProtocolTrap = MD5
SNMPAuthPasswordTrap = authpwdread
SNMPPrivProtocolTrap = AES
SNMPPrivPasswordTrap = privpwdread
```

### Switch Configuration

Here is a switch configuration example in order to enable SNMP v3 in both directions on a Cisco Switch.

```
snmp-server engineID local AA5ED139B81D4A328D18ACD1
snmp-server group readGroup v3 priv
snmp-server group writeGroup v3 priv read v1default write v1default
snmp-server user readUser readGroup v3 auth md5 authpwdread priv aes 128
 privpwdread
snmp-server user writeUser writeGroup v3 auth md5 authpwdwrite priv aes 128
 privpwdwrite
snmp-server enable traps port-security
snmp-server enable traps port-security trap-rate 1
snmp-server host 192.168.0.50 version 3 priv readUser  port-security
```

## Command-Line Interface: Telnet and SSH

### Warning

Privilege detection is disabled in the current PacketFence version due to some issues (see #1370). So make sure that the **cliUser** and **cliPwd** you provide always get you into a privileged mode (except for Trapeze hardware).

PacketFence needs sometimes to establish an interactive command-line session with a switch. This can be done using Telnet. You can also use SSH. In order to do so, edit the switch configuration file (`/usr/local/pf/conf/switches.conf`) and set the following parameters:

```
cliTransport = SSH (or Telnet)
cliUser = admin
cliPwd = admin_pwd
cliEnablePwd =
```

It can also be done through the Web Administration Interface under **Configuration → Policies and Access Control → Switches**.

## Web Services Interface

PacketFence sometimes needs to establish a dialog with the Web Services capabilities of a switch. In order to do so, edit the switch config file (`/usr/local/pf/conf/switches.conf`) and set the following parameters:

```
wsTransport = http (or https)
wsUser = admin
wsPwd = admin_pwd
```

It can also be done through the Web Administration Interface under **Configuration → Policies and Access Control → Switches**.

## Role-based enforcement support

Some network devices support the assignment of a specific set of rules (firewall or ACLs) to a user. The idea is that these rules can be a lot more accurate to control what a user can or cannot do compared to VLAN which have a larger network management overhead.

PacketFence supports assigning roles on devices for switches and WiFi controllers that support it. The current role assignment strategy is to assign it along with the VLAN (that may change in the future). A special internal role to external role assignment must be configured in the switch configuration file (`/usr/local/pf/conf/switches.conf`).

The current format is the following:

```
Format: <rolename>Role=<controller_role>
```

And you assign it to the global `roles` parameter or the per-switch one. For example:

```
adminRole=full-access
engineeringRole=full-access
salesRole=little-access
```

would return the `full-access` role to the nodes categorized as admin or engineering and the role `little-access` to nodes categorized as sales. It can also be done through the Web Administration Interface under **Configuration → Policies and Access Control → Switches**.

### Caution

Make sure that the roles are properly defined on the network devices prior to assigning roles!

## Connection Profiles

PacketFence comes with a default connection profile. The follow parameters are important to configure no matter if you use the default connection profile or create a new one:

- Redirect URL under **Configuration → Policies and Access Control → Connection Profile → Profile Name**

For some browsers, it is preferable to redirect the user to a specific URL instead of the URL the user originally intended to visit. For these browsers, the URL defined in `redirecturl` will be the one where the user will be redirected. Affected browsers are Firefox 3 and later.

- IP under **Configuration → Advanced Access Configuration → Captive portal**

This IP is used as the web server who hosts the `common/network-access-detection.gif` which is used to detect if network access was enabled. It cannot be a domain name since it is used in registration or quarantine where DNS is black-holed. It is recommended that you allow your users to reach your PacketFence server and put your LAN's PacketFence IP. By default we will make this reach PacketFence's website as an easier and more accessible solution.

In some cases, you may want to present a different captive portal (see below for the available customizations) according to the SSID, the VLAN, the switch IP/MAC or the URI the client connects to. To do so, PacketFence has the concept of connection profiles which gives you this possibility.

When configured, connection profiles will override default values for which it is configured. When no values are configured in the profile, PacketFence will take its default ones (according to the "default" connection profile).

Here are the different configuration parameters that can be set for each connection profiles. The only mandatory parameter is "filter", otherwise, PacketFence won't be able to correctly apply the connection profile. The parameters must be set in conf/profiles.conf:

```
[profilename1]
description = the description of your connection profile
filter = the name of the SSID for which you'd like to apply the profile, or the
 VLAN number
sources = comma-separated list of authentications sources (IDs) to use
```

Connection profiles should be managed from PacketFence's Web administrative GUI - from the **Configuration → Policies and Access Control → Connection Profiles** section. Adding a connection profile from that interface will correctly copy templates over - which can then be modified as you wish.

- Filters under **Configuration → Policies and Access Control → Connection Profile → Profile Name → Filters**

PacketFence offers the following filters: Connection Type, Network, Node Role, Port, realm, SSID, Switch, Switch Port, URI, VLAN and Time period.

Example with the most common ones:

- **SSID:** Guest-SSID
- **VLAN:** 100
- 
- **Switch Port:** <SwitchId>-<Port>
- **Network:** Network in CIDR format or an IP address

## Caution

Node role will take effect only with a 802.1X connection or if you use VLAN filters.

- Advanced filter under **Configuration → Policies and Access Control → Connection Profile → Profile Name → Advanced Filter**

Examples

- last_switch =~ "^JAMES" && extended.mse_inout.bob == "bobby"

PacketFence relies extensively on Apache for its captive portal, administrative interface and Web services. The PacketFence Apache configuration is located in `/usr/local/pf/conf/httpd.conf.d/`.

In this directory you have three important files: `httpd.admin`, `httpd.portal`, `httpd.webservices`, `httpd.aaa`.

- `httpd.admin` is used to manage PacketFence admin interface
- `httpd.portal` is used to manage PacketFence captive portal interface
- `httpd.webservices` is used to manage PacketFence webservices interface
- `httpd.aaa` is use to manage incoming RADIUS request

These files have been written using the Perl language and are completely dynamic - so they activate services only on the network interfaces provided for this purpose.

The other files in this directory are managed by PacketFence using templates, so it is easy to modify these files based on your configuration. SSL is enabled by default to secure access.

Upon PacketFence installation, self-signed certificates will be created in `/usr/local/pf/conf/ssl` (`server.key` and `server.crt`). Those certificates can be replaced anytime by your 3rd-party or existing wild card certificate without problems. Please note that the CN (Common Name) needs to be the same as the one defined in the PacketFence configuration file (`pf.conf`).

# Reuse 802.1X credentials

Under certain circumstances, for example to show an AUP after a successful 802.1X connection, it might be interesting to have the ability to use an "SSO emulation" in the sense that the user does not need to re-enter his credentials on the portal after having entered them during the 802.1X EAP process. The *Reuse 802.1X credentials* connection profile option will address this purpose. The same username as the one used during the 802.1X connection will be used against the different connection profile authentication sources to recompute the role from the portal.

As a security precaution, this option will only reuse 802.1X credentials if there is an authentication source matching the provided realm. This means, if users use 802.1X credentials with a domain part (username@domain, domain\username), the domain part needs to be configured as a realm under the RADIUS section and an authentication source needs to be configured for that realm. If users do not use 802.1X credentials with a domain part, only the NULL realm will be match IF an authentication source is configured for it.

# FreeRADIUS Configuration

This section presents the FreeRADIUS configuration steps. In some occasions, a RADIUS server is mandatory in order to give access to the network. For example, the usage of WPA2-Enterprise (Wireless 802.1X), MAC authentication and Wired 802.1X all require a RADIUS server to authenticate the users and the devices, and then to push the proper roles or VLAN attributes to the network equipment.

## Option 1: Authentication against Active Directory (AD)

### Caution

If you are using an Active/Active or Active/Passive cluster, please follow the instructions under *Option 1b* since the instructions below do not currently work in a cluster.

Go in the Administration interface under **Configuration → Policies and Access Control → Domains → Active Directory Domains**.

### Note

If you can't access this section and you have previously configured your server to bind to a domain externally to PacketFence, make sure you run `/usr/local/pf/addons/AD/migrate.pl`

Click **Add Domain** and fill in the information about your domain.

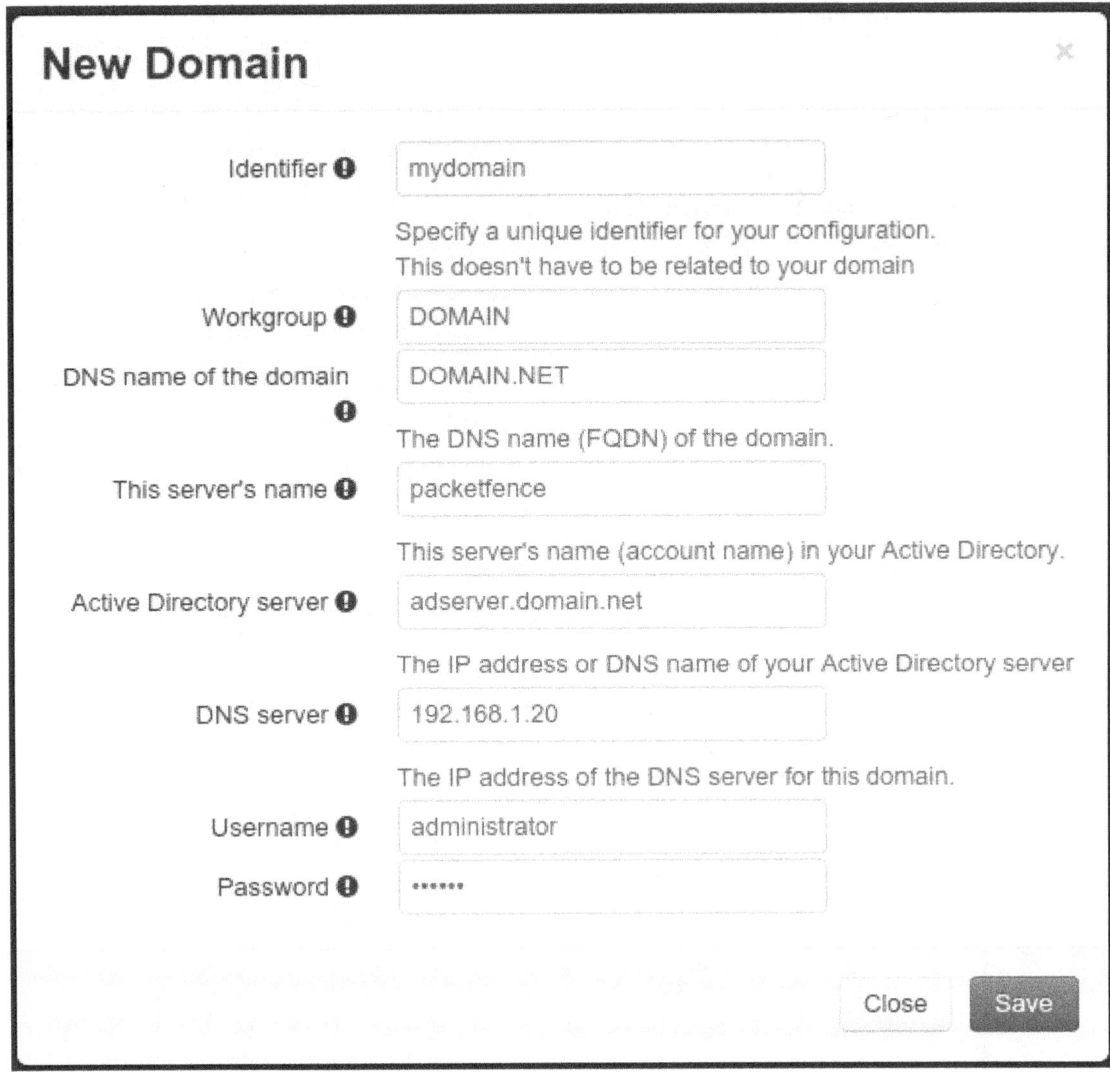


Where :

- **Identifier** is a unique identifier for your domain. It's purpose is only visual.
- **Workgroup** is the workgroup of your domain in the old syntax (like NT4).
- **DNS name of the domain** is the FQDN of your domain. The one that suffixes your account names.
- **This server's name** is the name that the server's account will have in your Active Directory.
- **DNS server** is the IP address of the DNS server of this domain. Make sure that the server you put there has the proper DNS entries for this domain.
- **Username** is the username that will be used for binding to the server. This account must be a domain administrator.
- **Password** is the password for the username defined above.

## Troubleshooting

- In order to troubleshoot unsuccessful binds, please refer to the following file : `/chroots/<mydomain>/var/log/samba<mydomain>/log.winbindd`. Replace `<mydomain>` with the identifier you set in the domain configuration.
- You can validate the domain bind using the following command : `chroot /chroots/<mydomain> wbinfo -u`
- You can test the authentication process using the following command `chroot /chroots/<mydomain> ntlm_auth --username=administrator`

Note

Under certain conditions, the test join may show as unsuccessful in the Administration interface but the authentication process will still work properly. Try the test above before doing any additional troubleshooting. Also try reloading the page in the GUI since in some case the browser side of the ajax call may time out while the join actually succeeds.

## Default domain configuration

You should now define the domain you want to use as the default one by creating the following realm in **Configuration → Policies and Access Control → Domains → REALMS**

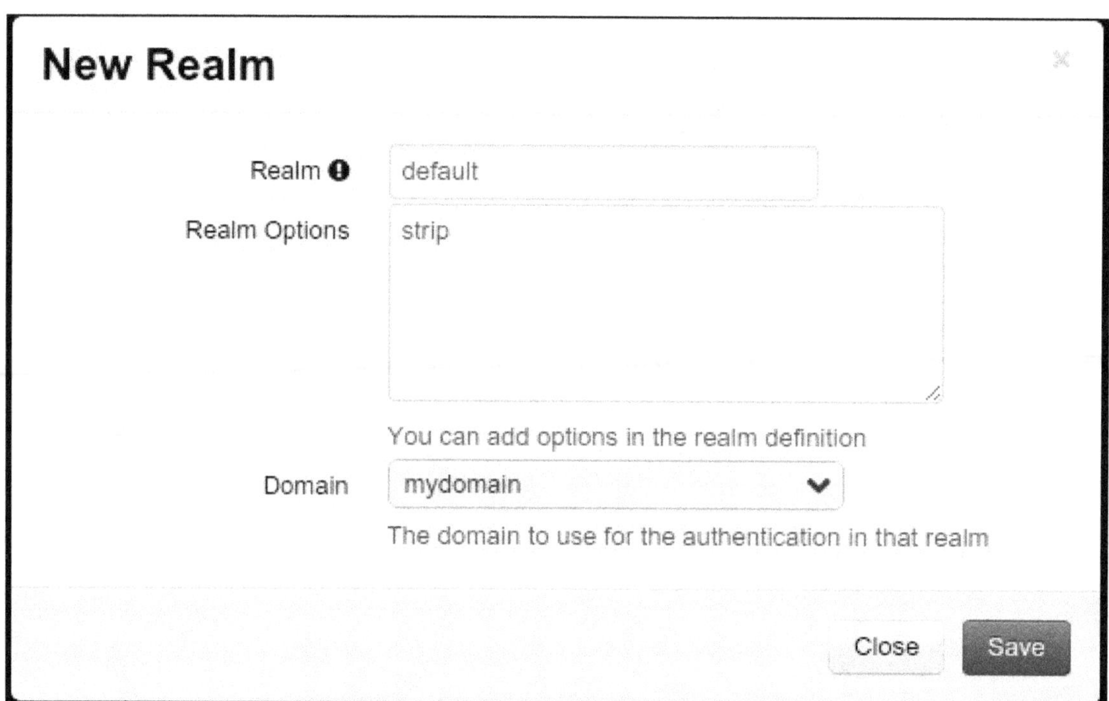


Next, restart PacketFence in **Status → Services**

## Multiple domains authentication

First configure your domains in **Configuration → Policies and Access Control → Domains → Active Directory Domains**.

Once they are configured, go in **Configuration → Policies and Access Control → Domains → REALMS**.

Create a new realm that matches the DNS name of your domain **AND** one that matches your workgroup. In the case of this example, it will be DOMAIN.NET and DOMAIN.

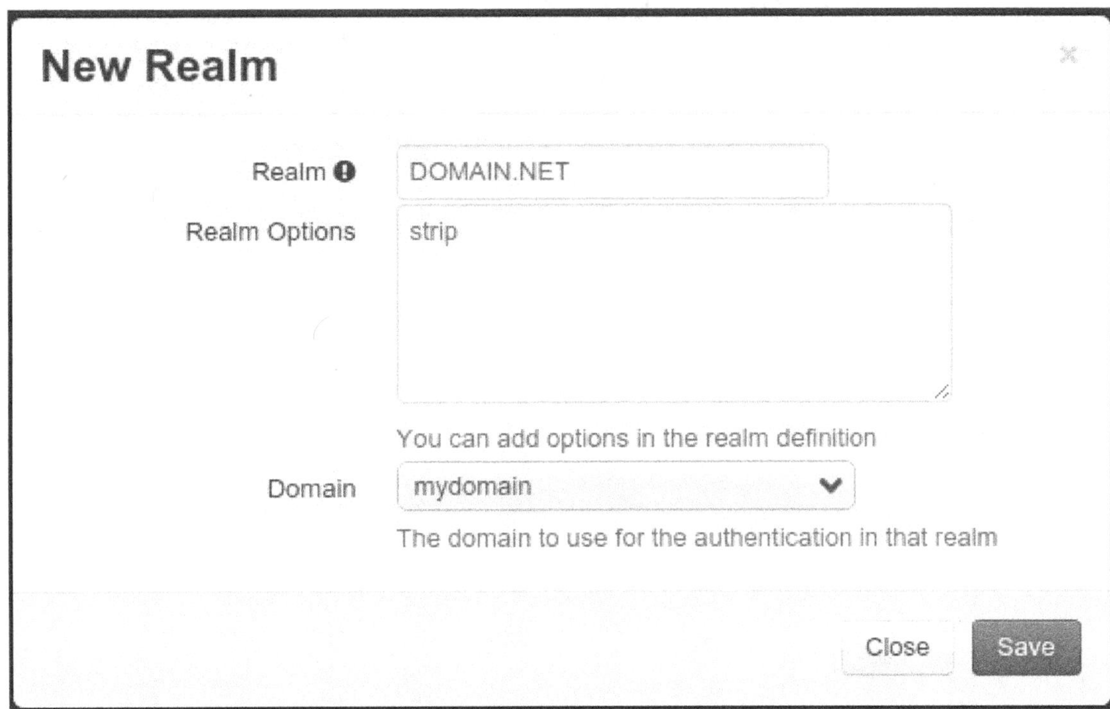


Where :

- **Realm** is either the DNS name (FQDN) of your domain or the workgroup
- **Realm options** are any realm options that you want to add to the FreeRADIUS configuration
- **Domain** is the domain which is associated to this realm

**Now create the two other realms associated to your other domains.**

You should now have the following realm configuration

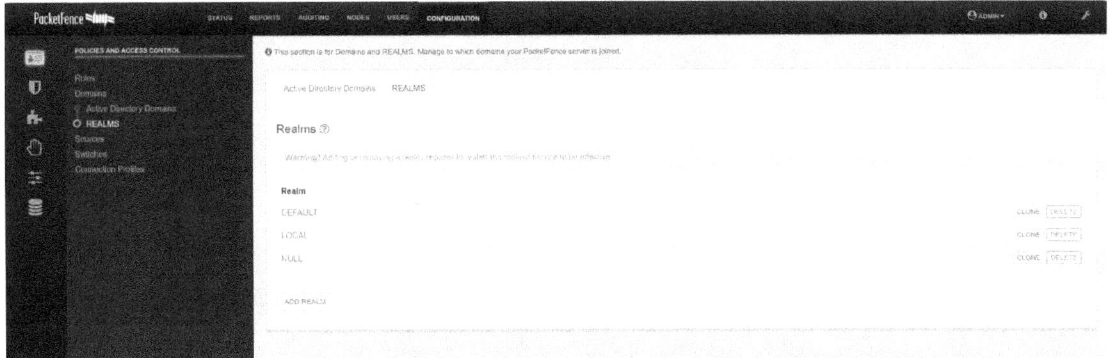

# Option 1b: Authentication against Active Directory (AD) in a cluster

## Samba / Kerberos / Winbind

Install Samba. You can either use the sources or use the package for your OS. For RHEL/CentOS, do:

```
yum install samba krb5-workstation
```

For Debian and Ubuntu, do:

```
apt-get install samba winbind krb5-user
```

Note

If you have Windows 7 PCs in your network, you need to use Samba version 3.5.0 (or greater).

When done with the Samba install, modify your `/etc/hosts` in order to add the FQDN of your Active Directory servers. Then, you need to modify `/etc/krb5.conf`. Here is an example for the `DOMAIN.NET` domain for CentOS/RHEL:

```
[logging]
 default = FILE:/var/log/krb5libs.log
 kdc = FILE:/var/log/krb5kdc.log
 admin_server = FILE:/var/log/kadmind.log

[libdefaults]
 default_realm = DOMAIN.NET
 dns_lookup_realm = false
 dns_lookup_kdc = false
 ticket_lifetime = 24h
 forwardable = yes

[realms]
 DOMAIN.NET = {
  kdc = adserver.domain.net:88
  admin_server = adserver.domain.net:749
  default_domain = domain.net
 }
[domain_realm]
 .domain.net = DOMAIN.NET
 domain.net = DOMAIN.NET

[appdefaults]
 pam = {
   debug = false
   ticket_lifetime = 36000
   renew_lifetime = 36000
   forwardable = true
   krb4_convert = false
 }
```

For Debian and Ubuntu:

```
[logging]
default = FILE:/var/log/krb5libs.log
kdc = FILE:/var/log/krb5kdc.log
admin_server = FILE:/var/log/kadmind.log
[libdefaults]
default_realm = DOMAIN.NET
ticket_lifetime = 24h
forwardable = yes
[appdefaults]
pam = {
debug = false
ticket_lifetime = 36000
renew_lifetime = 36000
forwardable = true
krb4_convert = false
}
```

Next, edit `/etc/samba/smb.conf`. Again, here is an example for our `DOMAIN.NET` for CentOS/RHEL:

```
[global]
workgroup = DOMAIN
server string = %h
security = ads
passdb backend = tdbsam
realm = DOMAIN.NET
encrypt passwords = yes
winbind use default domain = yes
client NTLMv2 auth = yes
preferred master = no
domain master = no
local master = no
load printers = no
log level = 1 winbind:5 auth:3
winbind max clients = 750
winbind max domain connections = 15
machine password timeout = 0
```

For Debian and Ubuntu:

```
[global]
workgroup = DOMAIN
server string = Samba Server Version %v
security = ads
realm = DOMAIN.NET
password server = 192.168.1.1
domain master = no
local master = no
preferred master = no
winbind separator = +
winbind enum users = yes
winbind enum groups = yes
winbind use default domain = yes
winbind nested groups = yes
winbind refresh tickets = yes
template homedir = /home/%D/%U
template shell = /bin/bash
client use spnego = yes
client ntlmv2 auth = yes
encrypt passwords = yes
restrict anonymous = 2
log file = /var/log/samba/log.%m
max log size = 50
machine password timeout = 0
```

Issue a **kinit** and **klist** in order to get and verify the Kerberos token:

```
# kinit administrator
# klist
```

After that, you need to start samba, and join the machine to the domain:

```
# service smb start
# chkconfig --level 345 smb on
# net ads join -U administrator
```

Note that for Debian and Ubuntu you will probably have this error:

```
# kinit succeeded but ads_sasl_spnego_krb5_bind failed: Invalid credentials
# Join to domain is not valid: Invalid credentials
```

For CentOS/RHEL:

```
# usermod -a -G wbpriv pf
```

Finally, start `winbind`, and test the setup using `ntlm_auth` and `radtest`:

```
# service winbind start
# chkconfig --level 345 winbind on
```

For Debian and Ubuntu:

```
# usermod -a -G winbindd_priv pf
# ntlm_auth --username myDomainUser
# radtest -t mschap -x myDomainUser myDomainPassword localhost:18120 12
 testing123
  Sending Access-Request of id 108 to 127.0.0.1 port 18120
      User-Name = "myDomainUser"
      NAS-IP-Address = 10.0.0.1
      NAS-Port = 12
      Message-Authenticator = 0x00000000000000000000000000000000
      MS-CHAP-Challenge = 0x79d62c9da4e55104
      MS-CHAP-Response =
 0x000100000000000000000000000000000000000000000000000091c843b420f0dec4228ed2f26bff07d5e49ad9a297
  rad_recv: Access-Accept packet from host 127.0.0.1 port 18120, id=108,
 length=20
```

## Option 2: Local Authentication

Add your user's entries at the end of the `/usr/local/pf/raddb/users` file with the following format:

```
username Cleartext-Password := "password"
```

## Option 3: EAP authentication against OpenLDAP

To authenticate 802.1X connection against OpenLDAP you need to define the LDAP connection in `/usr/local/pf/raddb/modules/ldap` and be sure that the user password is define as a NTHASH or as clear text.

```
        ldap openldap {
                server = "ldap.acme.com"
                identity = "uid=admin,dc=acme,dc=com"
                password = "password"
                basedn = "dc=district,dc=acme,dc=com"
                filter = "(uid=%{mschap:User-Name})"
                ldap_connections_number = 5
                timeout = 4
                timelimit = 3
                net_timeout = 1
                tls {
                }
                dictionary_mapping = ${confdir}/ldap.attrmap
                edir_account_policy_check = no

                keepalive {
                        # LDAP_OPT_X_KEEPALIVE_IDLE
                        idle = 60

                        # LDAP_OPT_X_KEEPALIVE_PROBES
                        probes = 3

                        # LDAP_OPT_X_KEEPALIVE_INTERVAL
                        interval = 3
                }
        }
```

Next in `/usr/local/pf/raddb/sites-available/packetfence-tunnel` add in the authorize section:

```
authorize {
        suffix
        ntdomain
        eap {
                ok = return
        }
        files
        openldap
    }
```

## Option 4: EAP Guest Authentication on email, sponsor and SMS registration

This section will allow local credentials created during guest registration to be used in 802.1X EAP-PEAP connections.

First create a guest SSID with the guest access you want to use (Email, Sponsor or SMS, ...) and activate *Create local account* on that source.

At the end of the guest registration, PacketFence will send an email with the credentials for Email and Sponsor. For SMS the phone number and the PIN code should be used.

Note

This option doesn't currently work with the *Reuse dot1x credentials* option of the captive portal.

In `/usr/local/pf/conf/radiusd/packetfence-tunnel` uncomment the line `# packetfence-local-auth` and restart radiusd.

This will activate the feature for any local account on the PacketFence server. You can restrict which accounts can be used by commenting the appropriate line in `/usr/local/pf/raddb/policy.d/packetfence`. For example, if you would want to deactivate this feature for accounts created via SMS, you would have the following :

```
packetfence-local-auth {
    # Disable ntlm_auth
    update control {
        &MS-CHAP-Use-NTLM-Auth := No
    }
    # Check password table for local user
    pflocal
    if (fail || notfound) {
        # Check password table with email and password for a sponsor registration
        pfguest
        if (fail || notfound) {
            # Check password table with email and password for a guest
 registration
            pfsponsor
            if (fail || notfound) {
                # *Don't* check activation table with phone number and PIN code
                # pfsms <--- This line was commented out
                if (fail || notfound) {
                    update control {
                        &MS-CHAP-Use-NTLM-Auth := Yes
                    }
                }
            }
        }
    }
}
```

Note

For this feature to work, the users' passwords must be stored in clear text in the database. This is configurable via `advanced.hash_passwords`.

## Option 5: EAP Local user Authentication

The goal here is to use the local user to authenticate 802.1X device.

Edit `/usr/local/pf/conf/radiusd/packetfence-tunnel`

```
# Uncomment the following line to enable local PEAP authentication
packetfence-local-auth
```

Restart the radiusd service in order to apply the change.

/usr/local/pf/bin/pfcmd service radiusd restart

Caution

You will need to disable password hashing in the database for local authentication to work. In the administration interface, go in *Configuration → System Configuration → Main Configuration →Advanced* and set *Database passwords hashing method* to `plaintext` or `ntlm`. Don't use `bcrypt`.

### Tests

Test your setup with `radtest` using the following command and make sure you get an `Access-Accept` answer:

```
# radtest dd9999 Abcd1234 localhost:18120 12 testing123
Sending Access-Request of id 74 to 127.0.0.1 port 18120
  User-Name = "dd9999"
  User-Password = "Abcd1234"
  NAS-IP-Address = 255.255.255.255
  NAS-Port = 12
rad_recv: Access-Accept packet from host 127.0.0.1:18120, id=74, length=20
```

## Portal Modules

The PacketFence captive portal flow is highly customizable. This section will cover the *Portal Modules* which are used to define the behavior of the captive portal.

Note

When upgrading from a version that doesn't have the portal modules, the PacketFence Portal Modules configuration already comes with defaults that will fit most cases and offers the same behavior as previous versions of PacketFence. Meaning, all the available Connection Profile sources are used for authentication, then the available provisioners will be used.

First, a brief description of the available Portal Modules:

- Root: This is where it all starts, this module is a simple container that defines all the modules that need to be applied in a chained way to the user. Once the user has completed all modules contained in the Root, he is released on the network.

- Choice: This allows to give a choice between multiple modules to the user. The *default_registration_policy* is a good example of a choice that is offered to the user.
- Chained: This allows you to define a list of modules that a user needs to go through in the order that they are defined - ex: you want your users to register via Google+ and pay for their access using PayPal.
- Message: This allows you to display a message to the user. An example is available below in *Displaying a message to the user after the registration*
- URL: This allows you to redirect the user to a local or external URL which can then come back to the portal to continue. An example is available below in *Calling an external website*.
- Authentication: The authentication modules can be of a lot of types. You would want to define one of these modules, in order to override the required fields, the source to use, the template or any other module attribute.
    - Billing: Allows to define a module based on one or more billing sources
    - Choice: Allows to define a module based on multiple sources and modules with advanced filtering options. See the section *Authentication Choice module* below for a detailed explanation.
    - Login: Allows you to define a username/password based module with multiple internal sources (Active Directory, LDAP, ...)
    - Other modules: The other modules are all based on the source type they are assigned to, they allow to select the source, the AUP acceptance, and mandatory fields if applicable.

# Examples

This section will contain the following examples:

- Prompting for fields without authentication.
- Prompting additional fields during the authentication.
- Chained authentication.
- Mixing login and Secure SSID on-boarding on the portal.
- Displaying a message to the user after the registration.

## Creating a custom root module

First, create a custom root module for our examples in order to not affect the default policy. In order to do so, go in *Configuration → Advanced Access Configuration → Advanced Access Configuration → Portal Modules*, then click *Add Portal Module* and select the type *Root*. Give it the identifier `my_first_root_module` and the description `My first root module`, then hit save.

Next, head to *Configuration → Policies and Access Control → Connection Profiles*, select the connection profile you use (most probably `default`) and then under *Root Portal Module*, assign `My first root module` then save your profile. If you were to access the captive portal now, an error would display since the Root module we configured doesn't contain anything.

You could add some of the pre-configured modules to the new Root module you created and that would make the error disappear.

## Prompting for fields without authentication

In order to prompt fields without authentication, you can use the Null source with the Null Portal Module.

PacketFence already comes with a Null source pre-configured. If you haven't modified it or deleted it, you can use it for this example. Otherwise, go in *Configuration → Policies and Access Control → Sources* and create a new Null source with a catchall rule that assigns a role and access duration.

Then go in *Configuration → Advanced Access Configuration → Advanced Access Configuration → Portal Modules* and click *Add Portal Module* and select *Authentication → Null*. Set the *Identifier* to **`prompt_fields`** and configure the module with the *Mandatory fields* you want and uncheck *Require AUP* so that the user doesn't have to accept the AUP before submitting these fields.

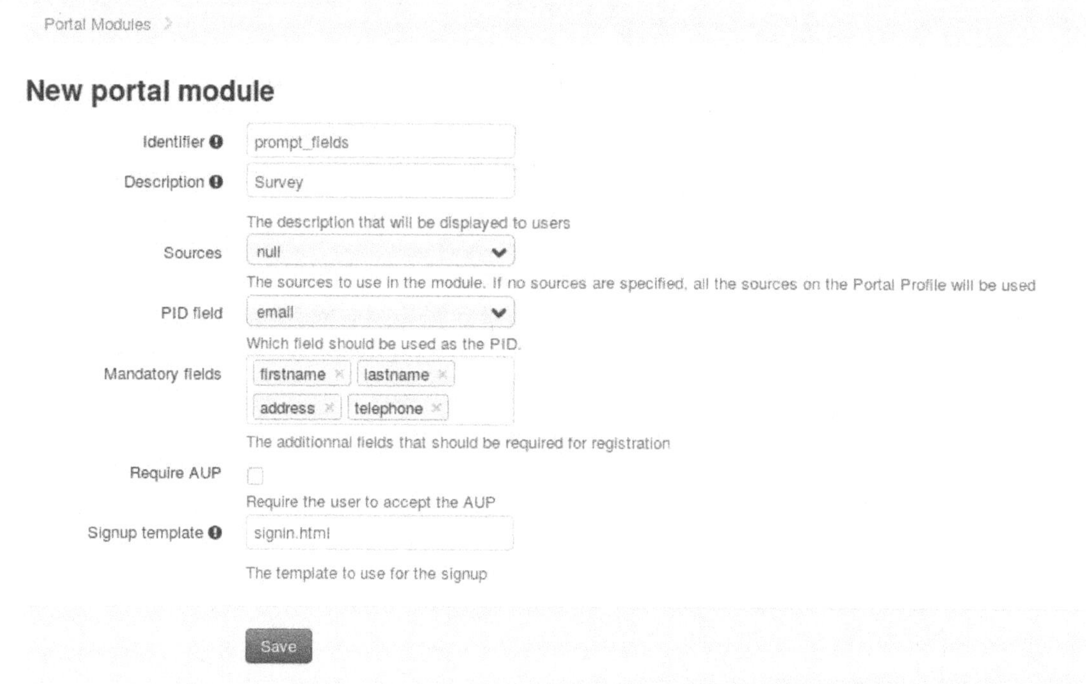


Next, add the **`prompt_fields`** module in **`my_first_root_module`** (removing any previous modules) and save it. Now when visiting the portal, it should prompt you for the fields you define in the module. Then, submitting these information will assign you the role and access duration that you defined in the **`null`** source.

## Prompting additional fields during the authentication

If you want to prompt additional fields during the authentication process for a module, you can define a Module based on that source that will specify the additional mandatory fields for this source.

You can also add additional mandatory fields to the default policies that are already configured.

This example will make the **`default_guest_policy`** require the user to enter a first name, last name and address so that guests have to enter these three information before registering.

Go in *Configuration → Advanced Access Configuration → Portal Modules* and click the **`default_guest_policy`**. Add **firstname**, **lastname** and **address** to the *Mandatory fields* and save.

Next, add the **default_guest_policy** to **my_first_root_module** (removing any previous modules). Now when visiting the portal, selecting any of the guest sources will require you to enter both the mandatory fields of the source (ex: phone + mobile provider) and the mandatory fields you defined in the **default_guest_policy**.

### Note

Not all sources support additional mandatory fields (ex: OAuth sources like Google, Facebook, ...).

## Chained authentication

The portal modules allow you to chain two or more modules together in order to make the user accomplish all of the actions in the module in the desired sequence.

This example will allow you to configure a *Chained* module that will require the user to login via any configured OAuth source (Github, Google+, ...) and then validate his phone number using SMS registration.

For the OAuth login we will use the **default_oauth_policy**, so just make sure you have an OAuth source configured correctly and available in your Connection Profile.

Then, we will create a module that will contain the definition of our SMS registration.

Go in *Configuration → Advanced Access Configuration → Portal Modules* then click *Add Portal Module* and select *Authentication → SMS*.

Configure the portal module so that it uses the **sms** source and uncheck the *Require AUP* option since the user will have already accepted the AUP when registering using OAuth.

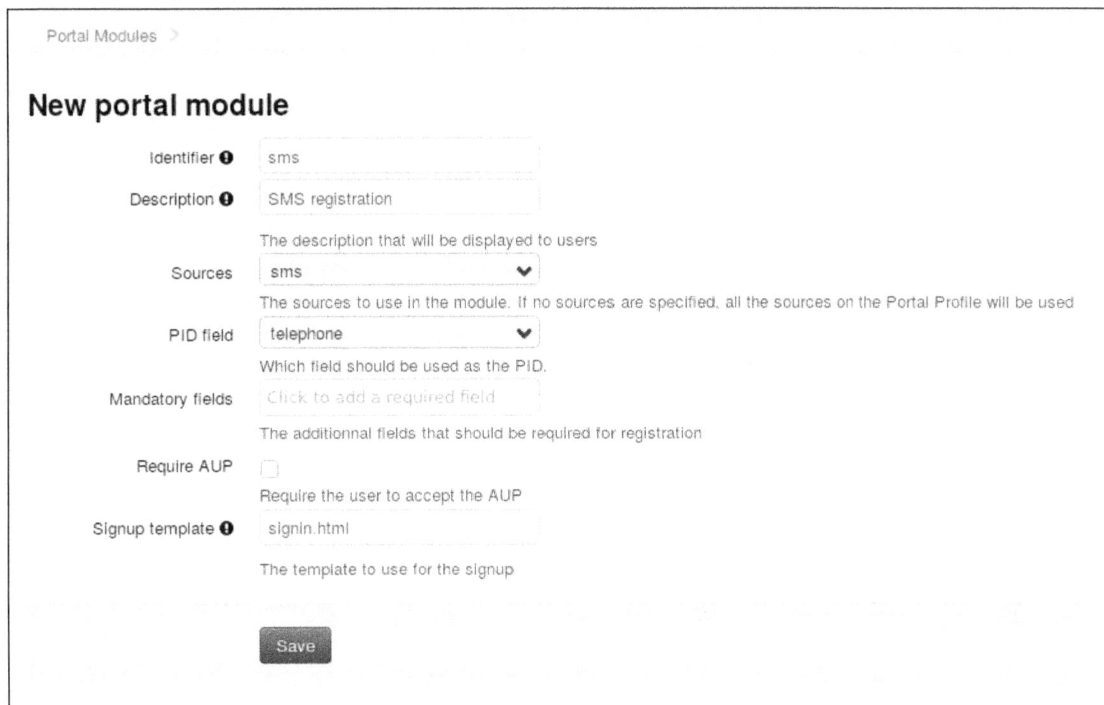


Then, add another Portal Module of type *Chained*. Name it **chained_oauth_sms**, assign a relevant description and then add **default_oauth_policy** and **sms** to the *Modules* fields

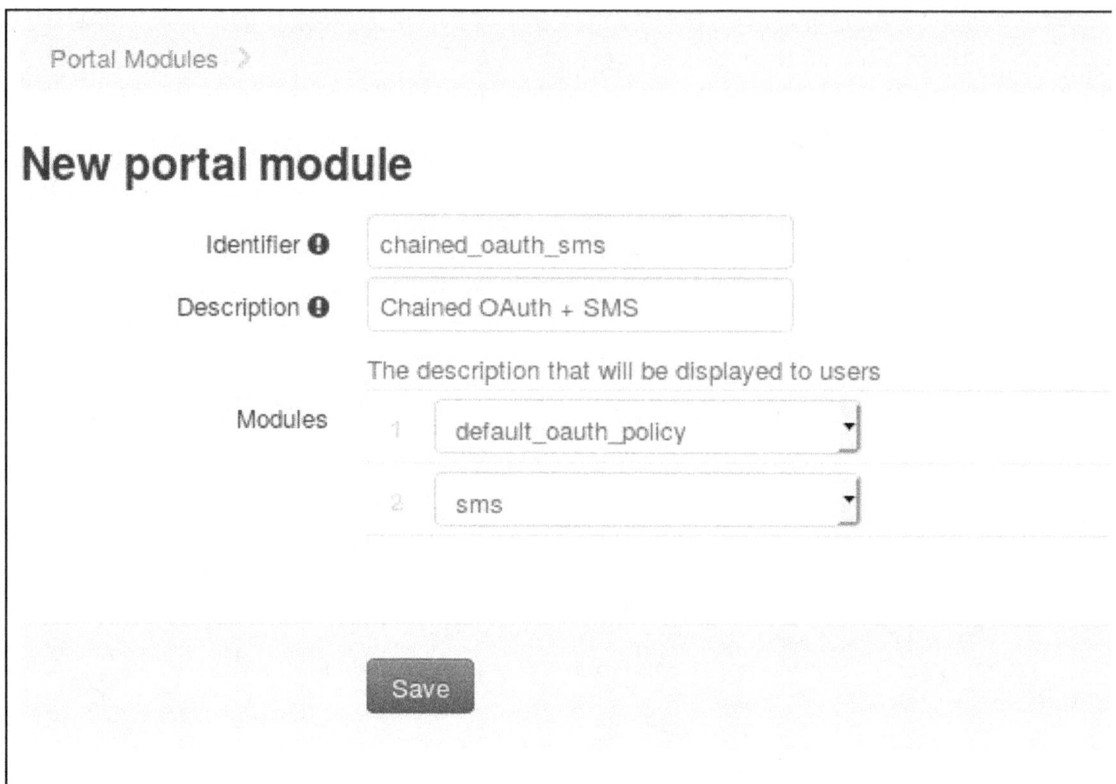


Next, add the `chained_oauth_sms` module in `my_first_root_module` (removing any previous modules) and save it. Now when visiting the portal, you should have to authentication using an OAuth source and then using SMS based registration.

## Mixing login and Secure SSID on-boarding on the portal

This example will guide you through configuring a portal flow that will allow for devices to access an open SSID using an LDAP username/password but also give the choice to configure the Secure SSID directly from the portal.

First, we need to configure the provisioners for the Secure SSID onboarding. Refer to section *Apple and Android Wireless Provisioning* of this guide to configure your provisioners and add them to the connection profile.

Create a provisioner of the type `Deny` and add it with your other provisioners (putting any other provisioner before it). This will make sure that if there is no match on the other provisioners, it will not allow the device through.

Also in the connection profile add your LDAP source to the available sources so its the only one available.

Next, create a *Provisioning* portal module by going in *Configuration → Advanced Access Configuration → Portal Modules*. Set the *Identifier* to `secure_boarding` and the description to `Board Secure SSID`. Also uncheck *Skippable* so the user is forced to board the SSID should it choose this option.

Then, still in the Portal Modules, create a *Choice* module. Set the *Identifier* to `login_or_boarding` and description to *Login or Boarding*. Add `secure_boarding` and `default_login_policy` to the *Modules* field and save.

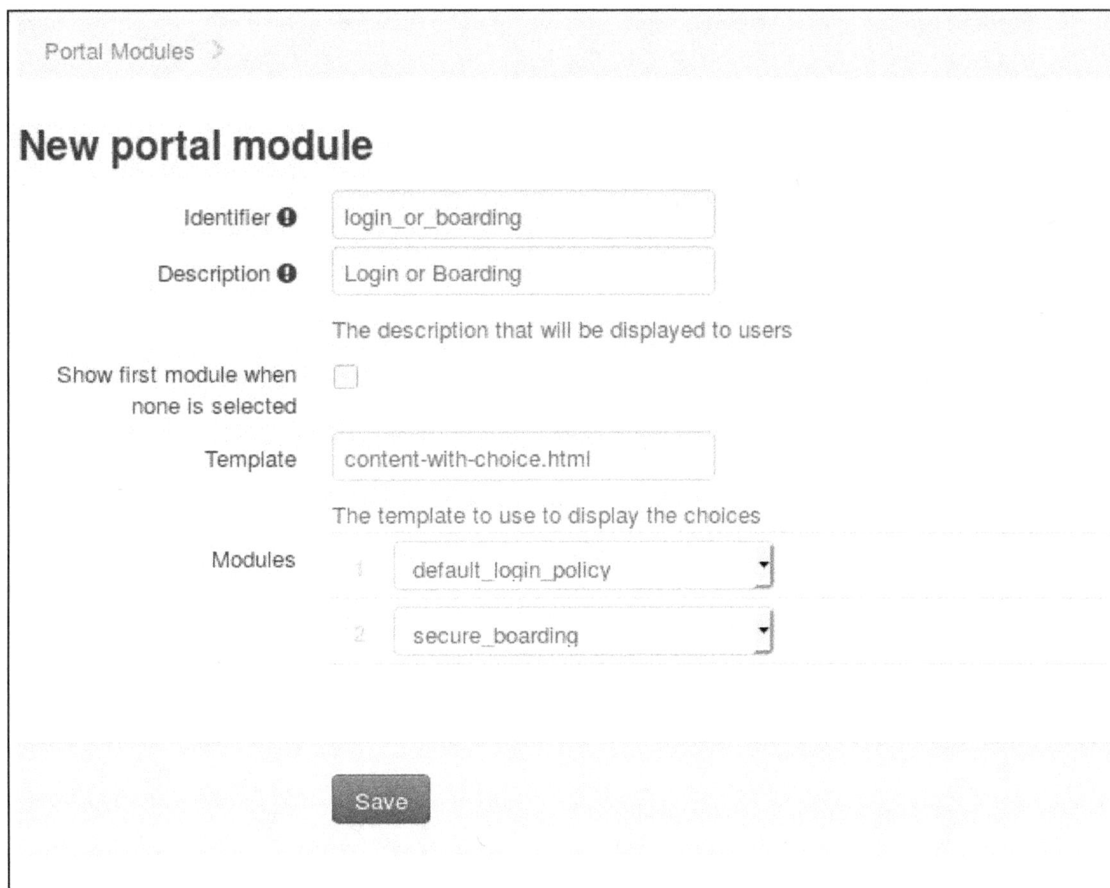


Next, add the `login_or_boarding` module in `my_first_root_module` (removing any previous modules) and save it. Now when visiting the portal, you will have the choice between login to the LDAP source and gain access to the network or directly use provisioning in order to configure your device for a Secure SSID.

Displaying a message to the user after the registration =

Using the *Message* module you can display a custom message to the user. You can also customize the template to display in order to display a fully custom page.

Go in *Configuration* → *Advanced Access Configuration* → *Portal Modules*, then click *Add Portal Module* and select *Message*. Set the *Identifier* to `hello_world` and the description to `Hello World`.

Then put the following in the *Message* field

```
Hello World !
<a href="www.packetfence.org">Click here to access the PacketFence website!</a>
```

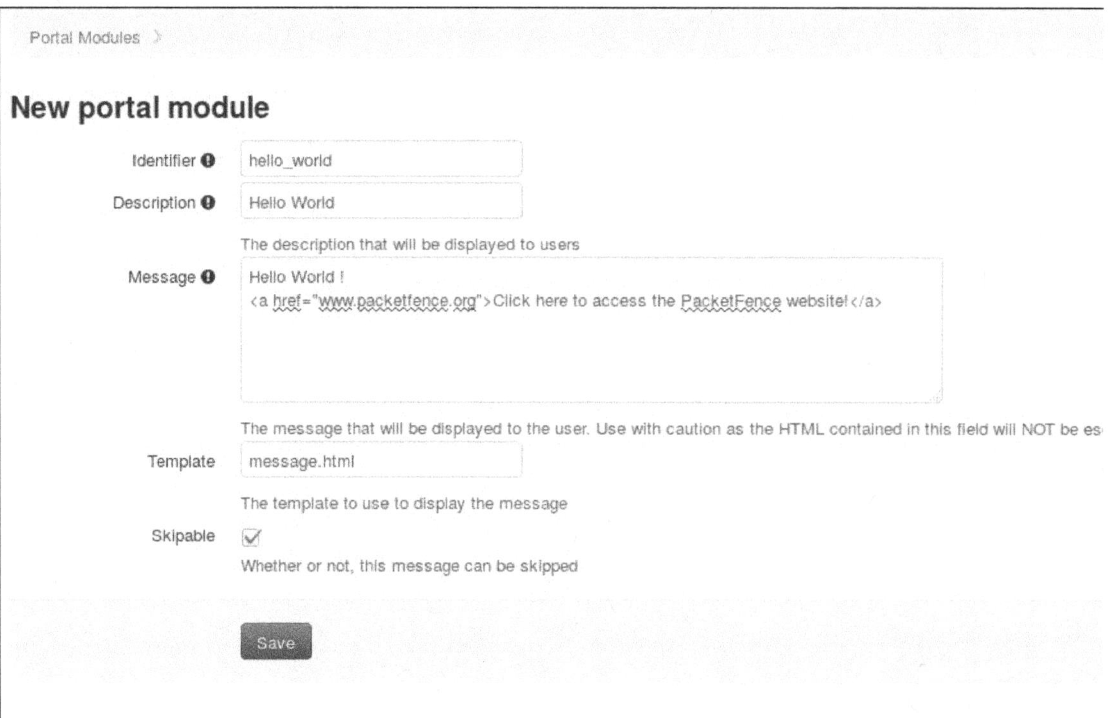


Next, add `default_registration_policy` and `hello_world` in the *Modules* of `my_first_root_module` (removing any previous modules) and save it. Now when visiting the portal, you should have to authenticate using the sources defined in your connection profile and you will then see the hello world message.

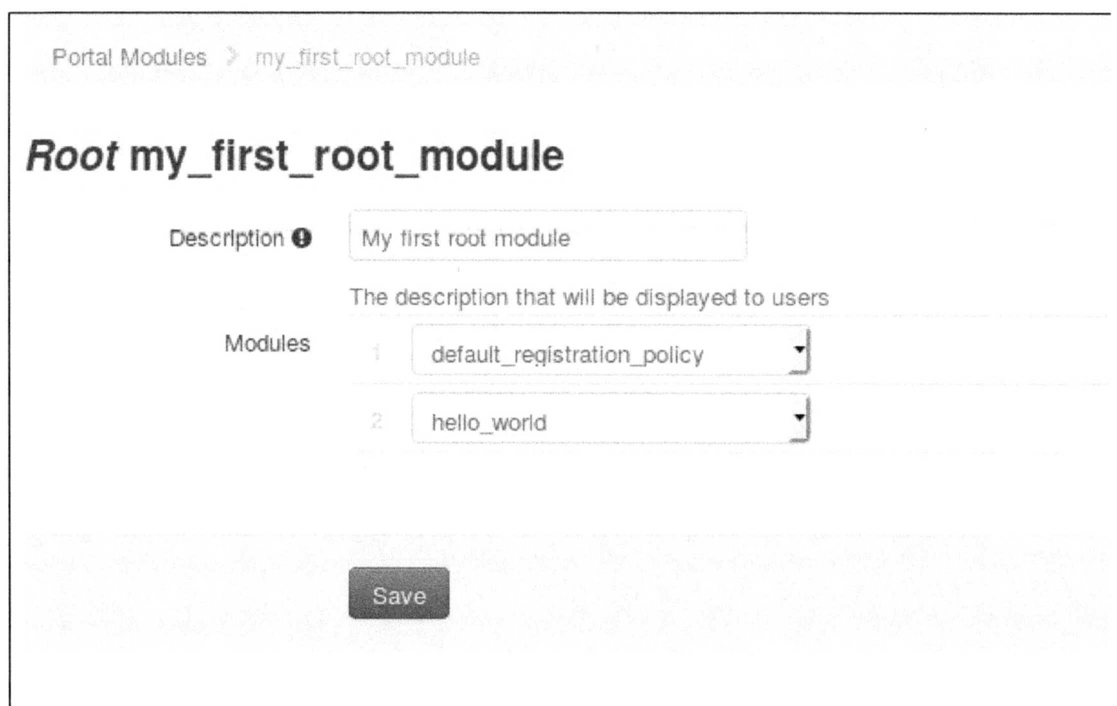

## Calling an external website

Using the *URL* module, you can redirect the user to a local or external URL (as long as it is in the passthroughs). Then you can make it so the portal accepts a callback in order for the flow to continue.

In this example, the portal will redirect to an externally hosted PHP script that will give a random token to the user and then callback the portal to complete the registration process.

The example script is located in `addons/example_external_auth/token.php` and a README is available in that directory to set it up.

Once you have the script installed and working on URL: `http://YOUR_PORTAL_HOSTNAME:10000/token.php`, you can configure what you need on the PacketFence side.

Go in *Configuration → Advanced Access Configuration → Portal Modules*, then click *Add Portal Module* and select *URL*. Set the *Identifier* to `token_system`, the *Description* to `Token system` and the *URL* to `http://YOUR_PORTAL_HOSTNAME:10000/token.php`.

Next, add `default_registration_policy` and `token_system` in the *Modules* of `my_first_root_module` (removing any previous modules) and save it. Now when visiting the portal, you should have to authenticate using the sources defined in your connection profile and then you will be redirected to example token system. Clicking the continue link on that system will bring you back to the portal and complete the registration process.

# Authentication Choice module (advanced)

The Authentication Choice module allows to define a choice between multiple sources using advanced filtering rules, manual selection of the sources and selection of Portal Modules.

All the sources that are defined in the *Sources* field will be available for usage by the user. Same goes for the modules defined in *Modules*.

You can also define which mandatory fields you want to prompt for these authentication choices. Although you can still configure them on any *Authentication Choice* module, they will only be shown if they are applicable to the source.

In addition to the manual selection above you can dynamically select sources part of the Connection Profile based on their object attribute (Object Class, Authentication type, Authentication Class).

### Note

You can find all the authentication objects in `lib/pf/Authentication/Source`

- Sources by class: Allows you to specify the perl class name of the sources you want available
  - ex: `pf::Authentication::Source::SMSSource` will select all the SMS sources. `pf::Authentication::Source::BillingSource` will select all the billing sources (Paypal, Stripe, ...)
- Sources by type: Allows you to filter out sources using the `type` attribute of the Authentication object

- Sources by Auth Class: Allows you to filter our sources using the `class` attribute of the Authentication object.

You can see the *default_guest_policy* and *default_oauth_policy* for examples of this module.

# Debugging

## Log files

Here are the most important PacketFence log files:

- `/usr/local/pf/logs/packetfence.log` — PacketFence Core Log
- `/usr/local/pf/logs/httpd.portal.access` — Apache - Captive Portal Access Log
- `/usr/local/pf/logs/httpd.portal.error` — Apache - Captive Portal Error Log
- `/usr/local/pf/logs/httpd.admin.access` — Apache - Web Admin/Services Access Log
- `/usr/local/pf/logs/httpd.admin.error` — Apache - Web Admin/Services Error Log
- `/usr/local/pf/logs/httpd.webservices.access` — Apache - Webservices Access Log
- `/usr/local/pf/logs/httpd.webservices.error` — Apache - Webservices Error Log
- `/usr/local/pf/logs/httpd.aaa.access` — Apache - AAA Access Log
- `/usr/local/pf/logs/httpd.aaa.error` — Apache - AAA Error Log

There are other log files in `/usr/local/pf/logs/` that could be relevant depending on what issue you are experiencing. Make sure you take a look at them.

The main logging configuration file is `/usr/local/pf/conf/log.conf`. It contains the configuration for the `packetfence.log` file (`Log::Log4Perl`) and you normally don't need to modify it. The logging configuration files for every service are located under `/usr/local/pf/conf/log.conf.d/`.

## RADIUS Debugging

First, check the FreeRADIUS logs. The file is located at `/usr/local/pf/logs/radius.log`.

If this didn't help, run FreeRADIUS in debug mode. To do so, start it using the following commands.

For the authentication radius process:

```
# radiusd -X -d /usr/local/pf/raddb -n auth
```

For the accounting radius process:

```
# radiusd -X -d /usr/local/pf/raddb -n acct
```

Additionally there is a **raddebug** tool that can extract debug logs from a running FreeRADIUS daemon. PacketFence's FreeRADIUS is pre-configured with such support.

In order to have an output from **raddebug**, you need to either:

a. Make sure user **pf** has a shell in **/etc/passwd**, add **/usr/sbin** to PATH (**export PATH=/usr/sbin:$PATH**) and execute **raddebug** as **pf**

b. Run **raddebug** as root (less secure!)

Now you can run **raddebug** easily:

```
raddebug -t 300 -f /usr/local/pf/var/run/radiusd.sock
```

The above will output FreeRADIUS' authentication debug logs for 5 minutes.

Use the following to debug radius accounting:

```
raddebug -t 300 -f /usr/local/pf/var/run/radiusd-acct.sock
```

See `man raddebug` for all the options.

# More on VoIP Integration

VoIP has been growing in popularity on enterprise networks. At first sight, the IT administrators think that deploying VoIP with a NAC poses a huge complicated challenge to resolve. In fact, depending of the hardware you have, not really. In this section, we will see why.

## CDP and LLDP are your friend

For those of you who are unaware of the existence of CDP or LLDP (or LLDP-MED), I suggest you start reading on this topic. Cisco Discovery Protocol (CDP) is device-discovery protocol that runs on all Cisco-manufactured equipment including routers, access servers, bridges, and switches. Using CDP, a device can advertise its existence to other devices and receive information about other devices on the same LAN or on the remote side of a WAN. In the world of VoIP, CDP is able to determine if the connecting device is an IP Phone or not, and tell the IP Phone to tag its ethernet frame using the configured voice VLAN on the switchport.

On many other vendors, you are likely to find LLDP or LLDP-MED support. Link Layer Discovery Protocol (LLDP) is a vendor-neutral Link Layer protocol in the Internet Protocol Suite used by network devices for advertising their identity, capabilities, and neighbors. Same as CDP, LLDP can tell an IP Phone which VLAN id is the voice VLAN.

## VoIP and VLAN assignment techniques

As you already know, PacketFence supports many VLAN assignment techniques such as port-security, mac authentication or 802.1X. Let's see how VoIP is doing with each of those.

### Port-security

Using port-security, the VoIP device rely on CDP/LLDP to tag its ethernet frame using the configured voice VLAN on the switch port. After that, we ensure that a security trap is sent from the voice VLAN so that PacketFence can authorize the mac address on the port. When the PC connects, another security trap will be sent, but from the data VLAN. That way, we will have 1 mac address authorized on the voice VLAN, and 1 on the access VLAN.

Note

Not all vendors support VoIP on port-security, please refer to the Network Configuration Guide.

## MAC Authentication and 802.1X

### Cisco hardware

On Cisco switches, we are looking at the multi-domain configuration. The multi-domain means that we can have one device on the VOICE domain, and one device on the DATA domain. The domain assignment is done using a Cisco Vendor-Specific Attributes (VSA). When the phone connects to the switchport, PacketFence will respond with the proper VSA only, no RADIUS tunneled attributes. CDP then tells the phone to tag its ethernet frames using the configured voice VLAN on the port. When a PC connects, the RADIUS server will return tunneled attributes, and the switch will place the port in the provided access VLAN.

### Non-Cisco hardware

On other vendor hardware, it is possible to make VoIP work using RADIUS VSAs. When a phone connects to a switchport, PacketFence needs to return the proper VSA to tell the switch to allow tagged frames from this device. When the PC will connect, we will be able to return standard RADIUS tunnel attributes to the switch, that will be the untagged VLAN.

Note

Again, refer to the Network Configuration Guide to see if VoIP is supported on your switch hardware.

# What if CDP/LLDP feature is missing

It is possible that your phone doesn't support CDP or LLDP. If it's the case, you are probably looking at the "DHCP way" of provisioning your phone with a voice VLAN. Some models will ask for a specific DHCP option so that the DHCP server can give the phone a voice VLAN id. The phone will then reboot, and tag its ethernet frame using the provided VLAN tag.

In order to make this scenario work with PacketFence, you need to ensure that you tweak the registration and your production DHCP server to provide the DHCP option. You also need to make sure there is a voice VLAN properly configured on the port, and that you auto-register your IP Phones (On the first connect, the phone will be assigned on the registration VLAN).

# Advanced topics

This section covers advanced topics in PacketFence. Note that it is also possible to configure PacketFence manually using its configuration files instead of its Web administrative interface. It is still recommended to use the Web interface.

In any case, the `/usr/local/pf/conf/pf.conf` file contains the PacketFence general configuration. For example, this is the place where we inform PacketFence it will work in VLAN isolation mode.

All the default parameters and their descriptions are stored in `/usr/local/pf/conf/pf.conf.defaults`.

In order to override a default parameter, define it and set it in `pf.conf`.

`/usr/local/pf/conf/documentation.conf` holds the complete list of all available parameters.

All these parameters are also accessible through the web-based administration interface under the Configuration tab. It is highly recommended that you use the web-based administration interface of PacketFence for any configuration changes.

## Apple, Android and Windows Wireless Provisioning

Apple devices such as iPhones, iPads, iPods and Mac OS X (10.7+) support wireless profile importation using a special XML file format (mobileconfig). Android is also able to support this feature by importing the wireless profile with the Android PacketFence Agent. In fact, installing such file on your Apple device will automatically configure the wireless settings for a given SSID. This feature is often used when the SSID is hidden, and you want to ease the configuration steps on the mobile device (because it is often painful to configure manually). In PacketFence, we are going further, we generate the profile according to the administrator's preference and we pre-populate the file with the user's credentials (without the password). The user simply needs to install its generated file and he will be able to use the new SSID.

The Windows agent will import and apply the provisioned profile so that the user only needs to enter his username and password.

# Configure the feature

Note

If EAP-TLS provisioning is desired, you have to configure a PKI before going any further. Two guides exists to assist you: *PacketFence PKI Quick Install Guide*, which covers PacketFence's implementation, or *PacketFence MSPKI Quick Install Guide* which covers Microsoft's.

First of all, you need to configure the SSID that your devices will use after they go through the authentication process.

In the administration interface, go in *Advanced Access Configuration* → *Provisioners*. Then select *android / ios / Windows* provisioner. Enter the SSID information and roles for which the provisioner applies. Repeat for all desired provisioners. Note that the default RADIUS certificate path is `/usr/local/pf/raddb/certs/server.crt`.

After, you simply need to add the *Android*, *iOS* and *Windows* provisioners to your *Connection Profile* configuration.

## Android specificities

For Android provisioning support, you must activate and adjust the passthroughs. You might need to adapt them depending on your geolocality. NOTE: Please refer to the *Passthroughs* section of this guide if needed.

In the administation inferface, go in *Network Configuration* → *Fencing*. Activate *Passthrough* and make sure the following passthrough are present:

```
*.ggpht.com,*.googleusercontent.com,android.clients.google.com,*.googleapis.com,*.android.cl
```

Then run the following commands so that passthroughs become effective:

```
/usr/local/pf/bin/pfcmd configreload hard
/usr/local/pf/bin/pfcmd service iptables restart
/usr/local/pf/bin/pfcmd service pfdns restart
```

## iOS specificities

Mac OS X/iOS require the provisioning profile to be signed if you want to remove the `untrusted` warning when installing the profile. For more information, please refer to the PKI guides referred earlier in *Configure the feature* above.

# Profile generation

Upon registration, instead of showing the default release page, the user will be showing another version of the page saying that the wireless profile has been generated with a clickable link on it.

To install the profile, Apple user owner simply need to click on that link, and follow the instructions on their device. Android user owner simply click to the link and will be forwarded to Google Play to install PacketFence agent. Simply launch the application and click to configure will create the secure SSID profile. It is that simple.

# Billing Engine

PacketFence integrates the ability to use a payment gateway to bill users to gain access to the network. When configured, the user who wants to access the network / Internet is prompted by a page asking for it's personal information as well as it's credit card information.

PacketFence currently supports four payment gateways: Authorize.net, Mirapay, Paypal and Stripe.

In order to activate the billing, you will need to configure the following components :

- Billing source(s)
- Billing tier(s)

## Configuring a billing source

First select a billing provider and follow the instructions below.

### Paypal

Note

This provider requires that your PacketFence server is accessible on the public domain. For this your PacketFence portal should be available on a public IP using the DNS server name configured in PacketFence.

If you have a business account and do not want to configure a test environment, you can skip the next section.

#### Sandbox account

To configure a sandbox paypal account for use in PacketFence, head to https://developer.paypal.com/ and either sign up or login into your existing account.

Then in the Sandbox menu, click *Accounts*

Create an account that has the type *Personal* and one that has the type *Business*.

Afterwards, go back into accounts, and expand the business account, then click *Profile*

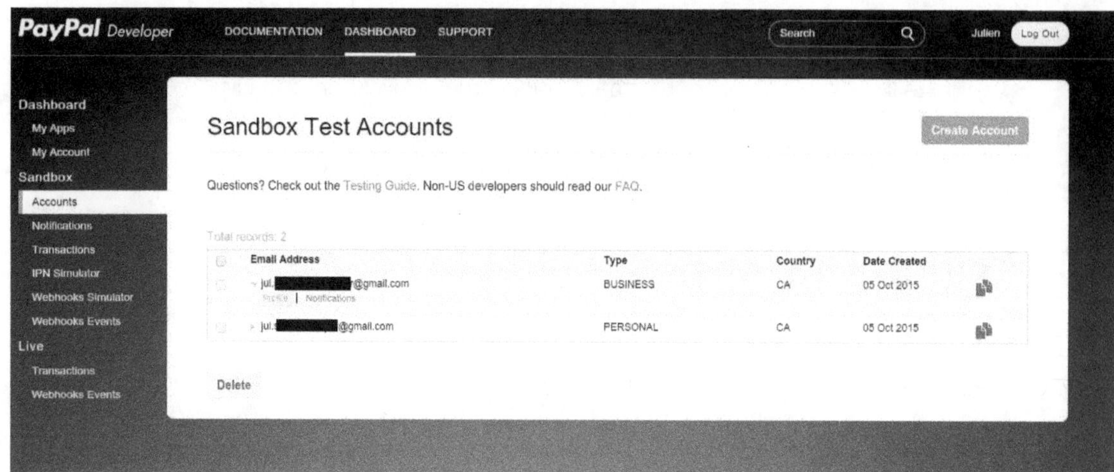


Now click the *Change password* link and change the password and note it.

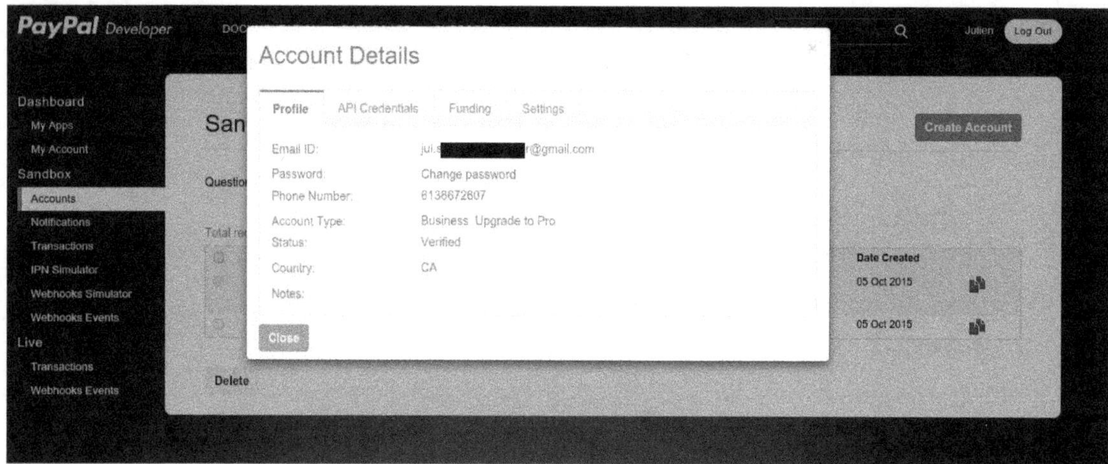


Do the same thing with the personal account you created

**Configuring the merchant account**

Login into the Paypal business account that you created at https://www.sandbox.paypal.com/ if you are using a sandbox account or on https://www.paypal.com/ if you are using a real account.

Next go in *My Account* → *Profile* in order to go into your profile configuration.

Next in the *Selling Preferences* you will need to select *Website Payment Preferences*

Configure the settings so they match the screenshot below.

You should turn on *Auto Return*, set the return URL to https://YOUR_PORTAL_HOSTNAME/billing/paypal/verify.

You should also take note of the *Identity Token* as it will be required in the PacketFence configuration.

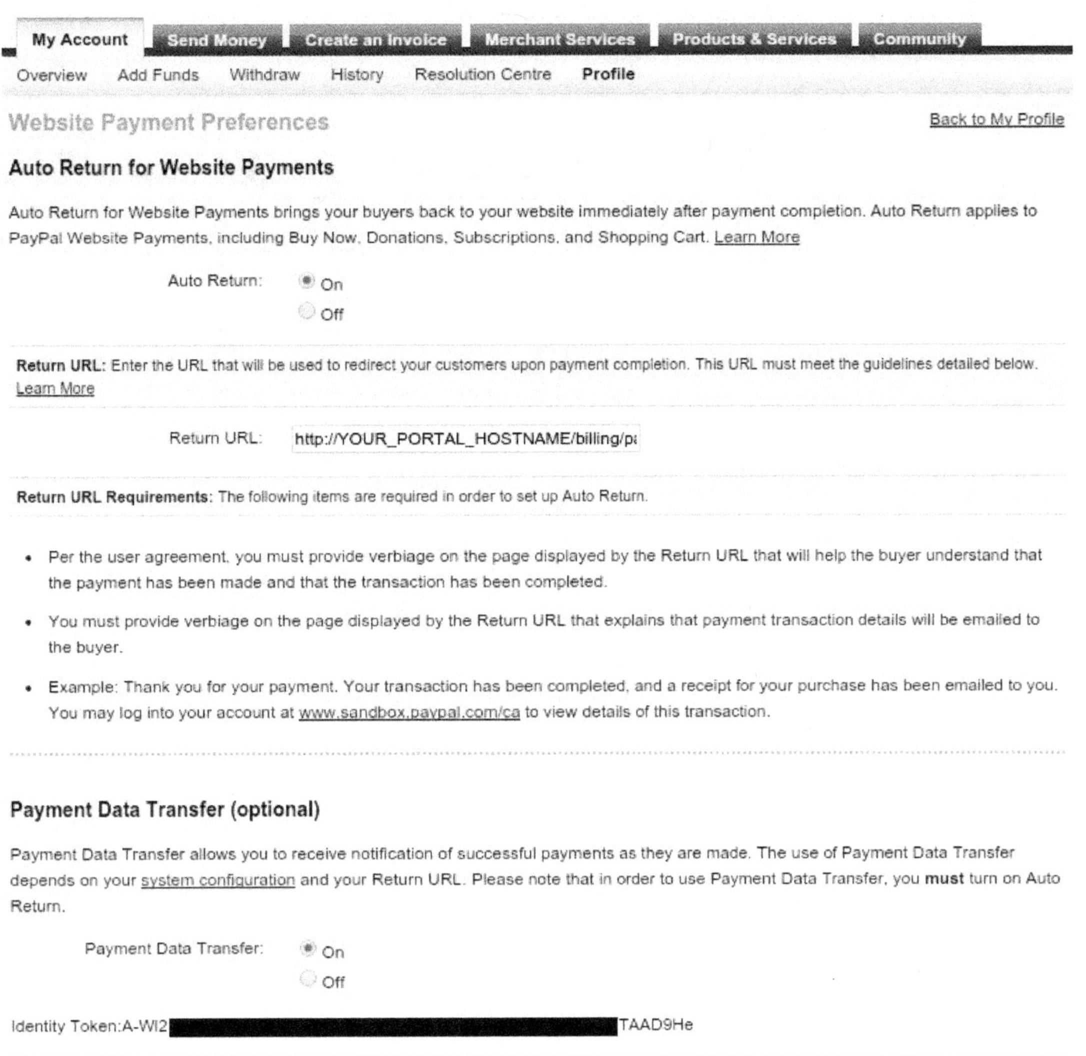


Next go back in your profile configuration *My account → Profile* and select *Encrypted Payment Settings*

Now on this page you will need to submit the certificate used by PacketFence to Paypal (/usr/local/pf/conf/ssl/server.crt by default).

Once you have submitted it, note it's associated *Cert ID* as you will need to configure it in PacketFence.

Still on that page, click the *Download* link to download the Paypal public certificate and put it on the PacketFence server under path : /usr/local/pf/conf/ssl/paypal.pem

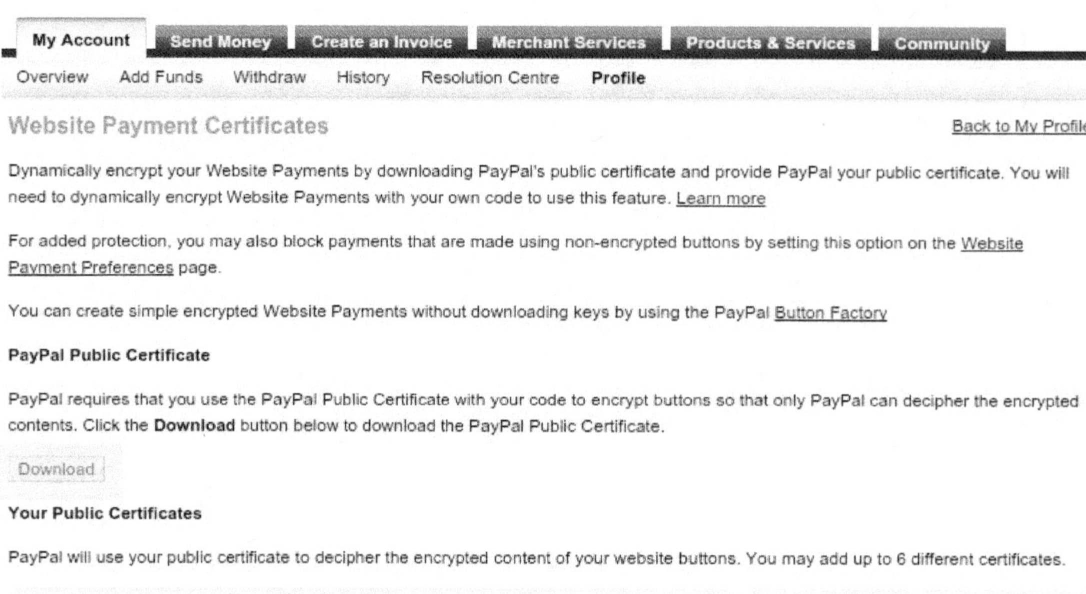

My Account
Send Money
Create an Invoice
Merchant Services
Products & Services
Community
Overview
Add Funds
Withdraw
History
Resolution Centre
Profile
Website Payment Certificates
Back to My Profile
Dynamically encrypt your Website Payments by downloading PayPal's public certificate and provide PayPal your public certificate. You will need to dynamically encrypt Website Payments with your own code to use this feature. Learn more
For added protection, you may also block payments that are made using non-encrypted buttons by setting this option on the Website Payment Preferences page.
You can create simple encrypted Website Payments without downloading keys by using the PayPal Button Factory
PayPal Public Certificate
PayPal requires that you use the PayPal Public Certificate with your code to encrypt buttons so that only PayPal can decipher the encrypted contents. Click the Download button below to download the PayPal Public Certificate.
Download
Your Public Certificates
PayPal will use your public certificate to decipher the encrypted content of your website buttons. You may add up to 6 different certificates.
Cert ID
Certifying Authority
Expiration Date
VNG
/C=CA/ST=QC/L=Montreal/O=Inverse/CN=127.0.0.1/emailAddress=support@inverse.ca
May 14, 2016 21:59:11 GMT-04:00
Download
Remove
Add
About Us | Contact Us | Legal Agreements | Privacy | Fees | Site Feedback [-]
Copyright © 1999-2015 PayPal. All rights reserved.

### Caution

The certificate will **NOT** be the same if you use a sandbox account or a real account.

### Configuring PacketFence

Now, in the PacketFence administration interface, go in *Configuration→Policies and Access Control→Sources* and create a new source of type *Billing → Paypal*.

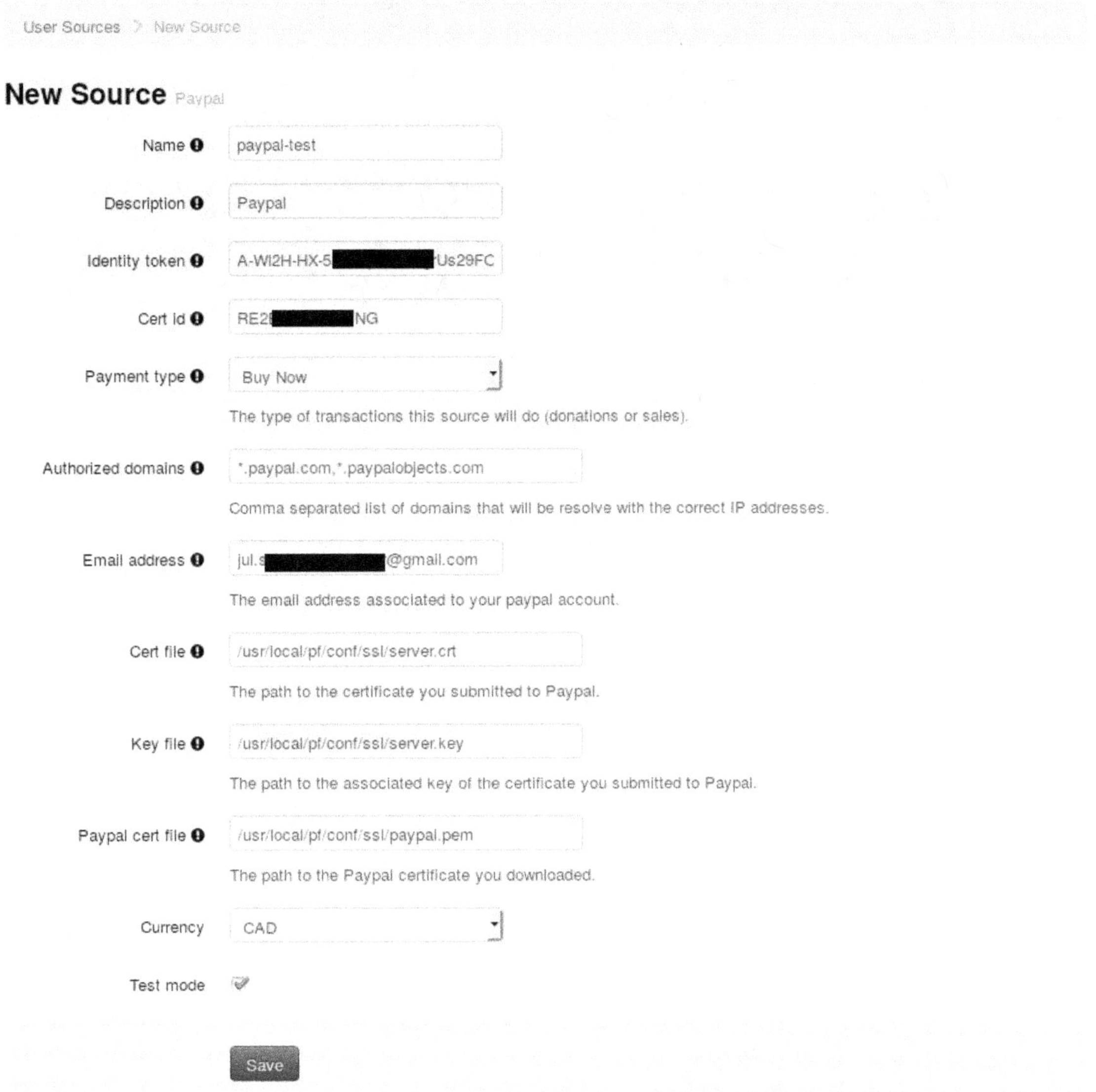


Where :

- **Identity token** is the one you noted when on the *Website Payment Preferences* page.
- **Cert ID** is the one you noted when on the *Encrypted Payment Settings*.
- **Payment type** is whether the access is donation based (not mandatory to pay for it).
- **Email address** is the email address of the merchant paypal account.
- **Cert file** is the path to the PacketFence certificate (/usr/local/pf/conf/ssl/server.crt by default).
- **Key file** is the path to the PacketFence certificate (/usr/local/pf/conf/ssl/server.key by default).
- **Paypal cert file** is the path to the Paypal certificate (/usr/local/pf/conf/ssl/paypal.pem in this example).
- **Currency** is the currency that will be used in the transactions.
- **Test mode** should be activated if you are using a sandbox account.

## Stripe

### Stripe account

First go on https://dashboard.stripe.com, create an account and login.

Next on the top right click *Your account* then *Account settings*.

Navigate to the *API keys* tab and note your key and secret. The test key should be used when testing the configuration and the live key when putting the source in production.

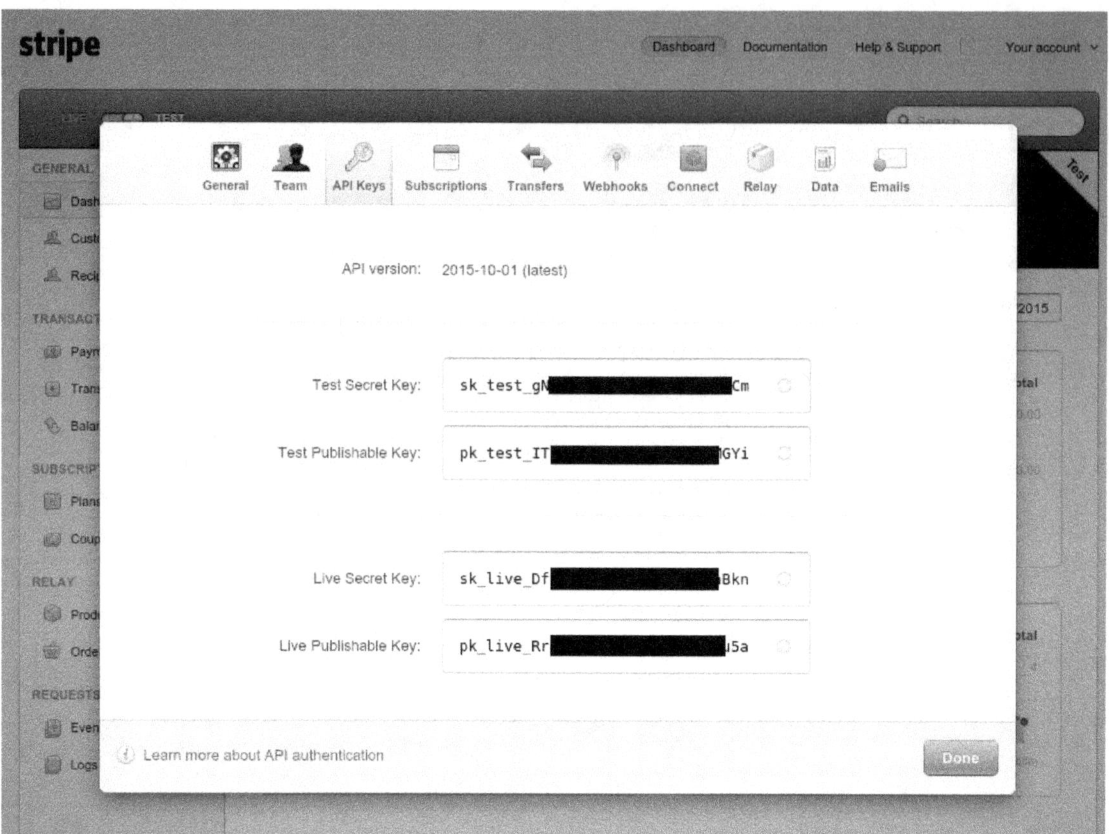


### Configuring PacketFence

Now, in the PacketFence administration interface, go in *Configuration→Policies and Access Control→Sources* and create a new source of type *Billing → Stripe*

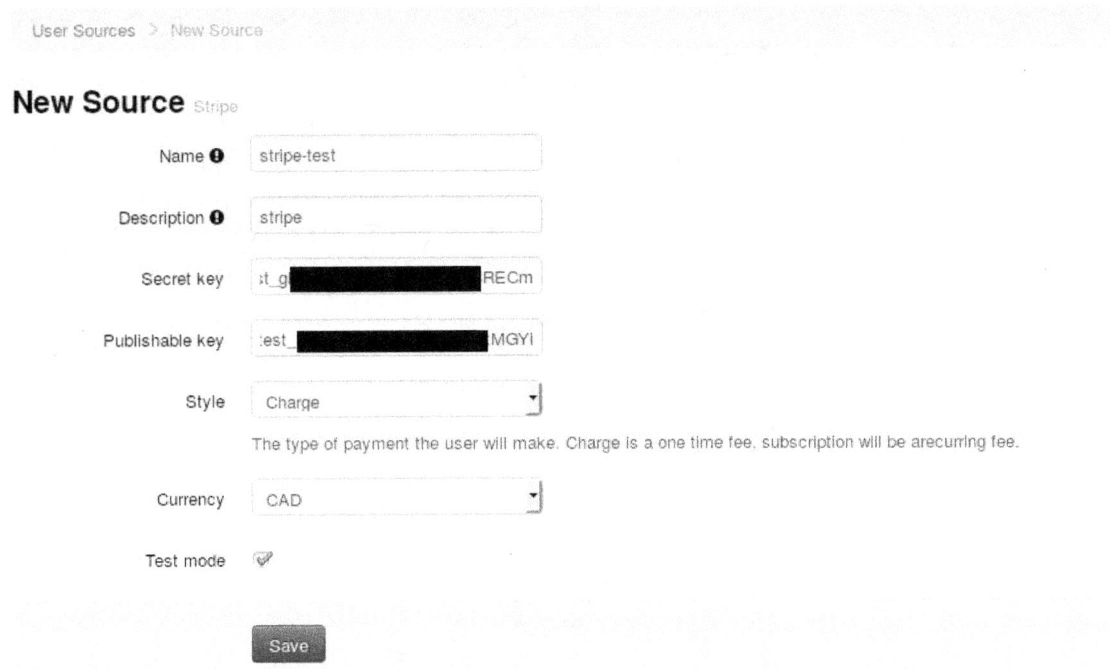


Where :

- **Secret key** is the secret key you got from your Stripe account.
- **Publishable key** is the publishable key you got from your Stripe account.
- **Style** is whether you are doing a one-time charge or subscription based billing (recurring). See section *Subscription based registration* below for details on how to configure it.
- **Currency** is the currency that will be used in the transactions.
- **Test mode** should be activated if you are using the test key and secret account.

## Authorize.net

### Creating an account

First go on https://account.authorize.net to signup for a merchant account or http://developer.authorize.net/ for a sandbox account.

After you created your account you will be shown your *API login ID* and *Transaction key*. Note both of these information for usage in the PacketFence configuration.

Then login into your new account.

Then under *Account* click *Settings*.

On the settings page in the section *Security settings*, click *MD5-Hash*

Now enter a secret that will be shared between authorize.net and PacketFence.

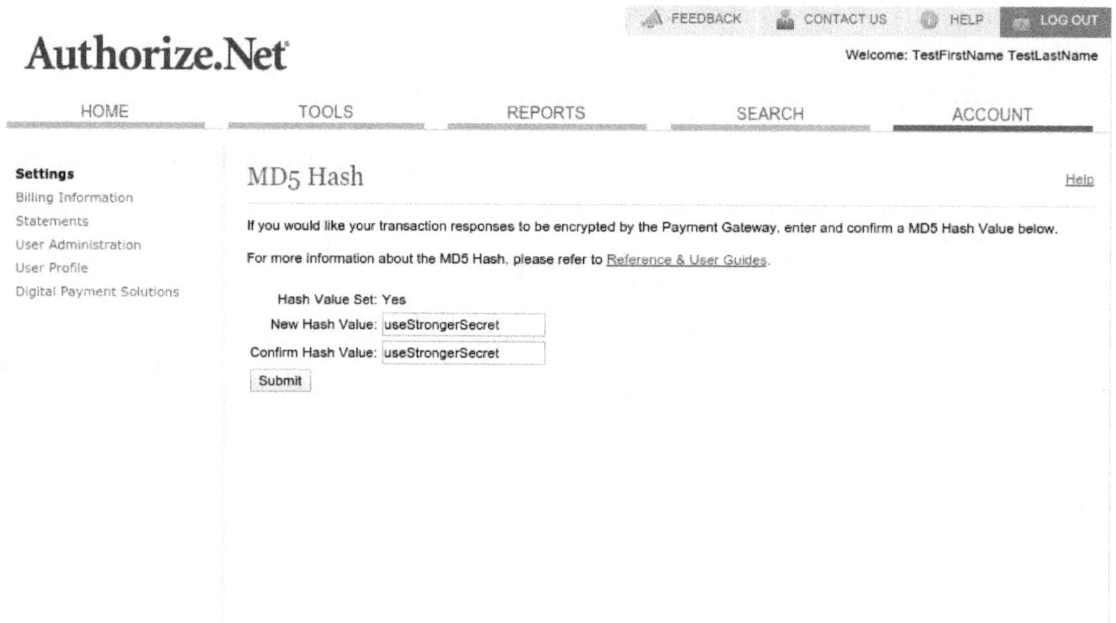


### PacketFence configuration

Next in the PacketFence administration interface, go in *Configuration→Policies and Access Control→Sources* and create a new source of type *Billing→AuthorizeNet*.

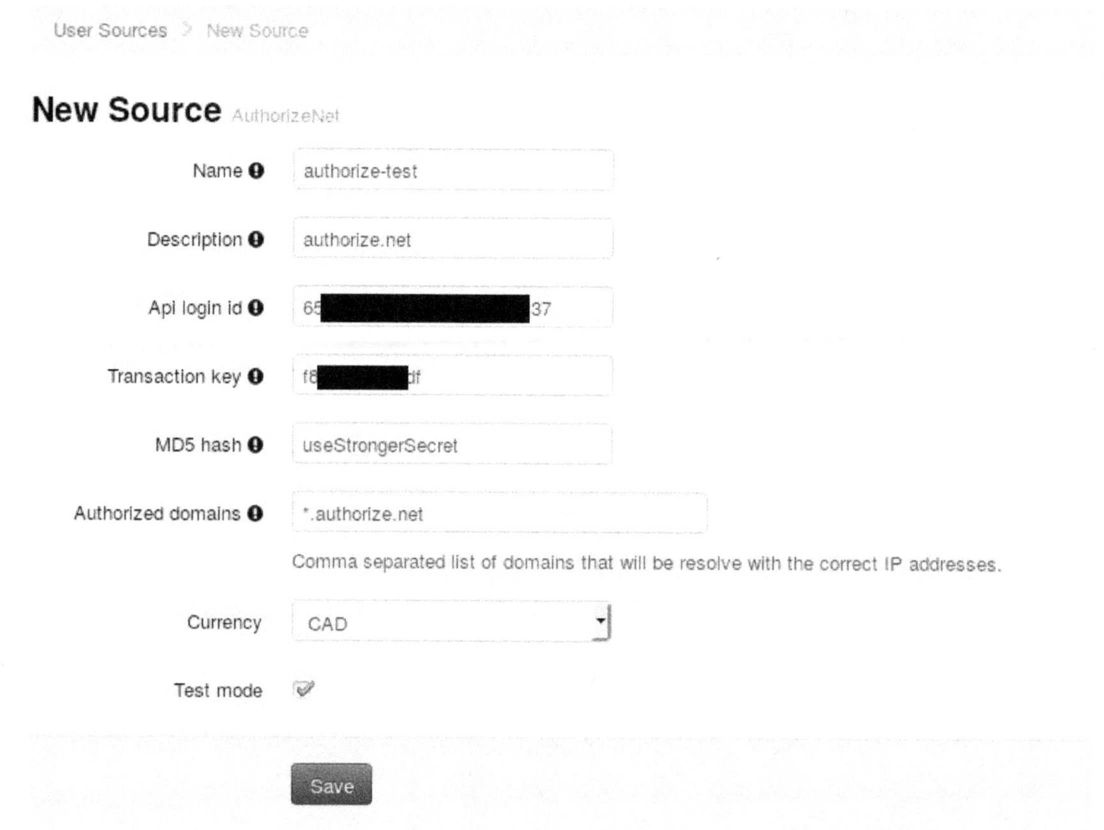


Where :

- **API login ID** is the one you got earlier while creating your account.
- **Transaction key** is the one you got earlier while creating your account.
- **MD5 hash** the one you configured in your Authorize.net account.
- **Currency** is the currency that will be used in the transactions.
- **Test mode** should be activated if you are using a sandbox account.

### Mirapay

```
To be contributed...
```

## Adding billing tiers

Once you have configured one or more billing source, you need to define billing tiers which will define the price and target authentication rules for the user.

In the PacketFence administration interface, go in *Configuration→Advanced Access Configuration→Billing tiers*

Then click *Add billing tier* and configure it.

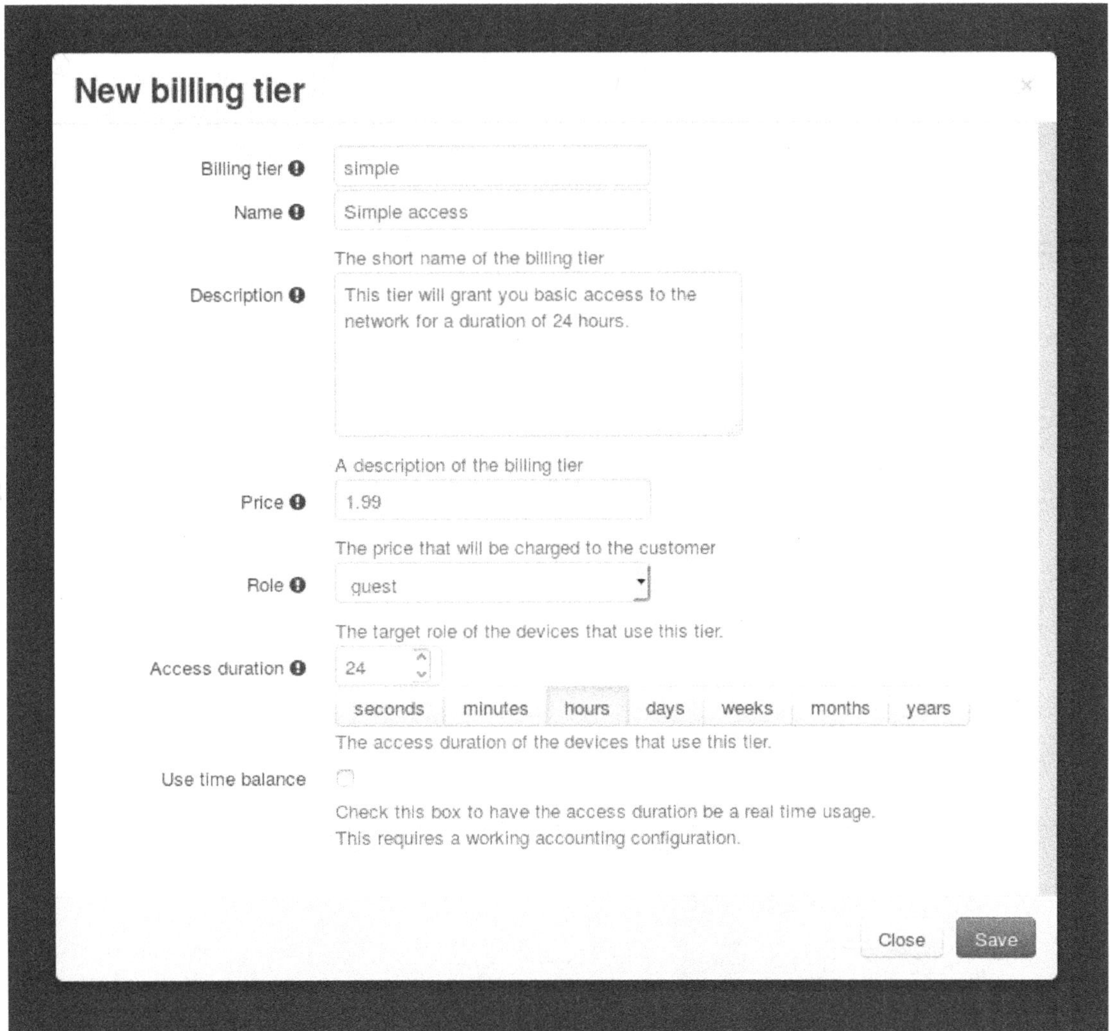

Where :

- **Billing tier** is the unique identifier of the billing tier.
- **Name** is the friendly name of the billing tier.
- **Description** is an extended description of the billing tier.
- **Price** is the amount that will be charged to the user.
- **Access duration** is the amount of time the user will be granted access to your network.
- **Role** is the target role the user should be in.
- **Use time balance** defines if the access duration should be computed on real-time access duration meaning if the user buys 24 hours of access he can use the network for 24 hours in different time blocks. This requires a valid RADIUS accounting configuration.

Note

If don't want to use all the billing tiers that are defined, you can specify the ones that should be active in the *Connection profile*.

## Subscription based registration

PacketFence supports subscription based billing using Stripe as a billing provider.

### Billing tier

When using subscription based billing, it is advised to configure the billing tier so it has an almost infinite access duration (e.g. 20 years) as the billing provider will be contacting the PacketFence server when the subscription is canceled.

You should configure a billing tier for each subscription plan you want to have. This example will use the plan *simple* and *advanced* configured using the following parameters.

```
[simple]
name=Simple network access
description=Click here if you are poor
price=3.99
role=guest
access_duration=10Y
use_time_balance=disabled
```

```
[advanced]
name=Simple network access
description=Click here if you are poor
price=9.99
role=advanced_guest
access_duration=10Y
use_time_balance=disabled
```

### Stripe configuration

Then in your Stripe dashboard, you should go in *Subscriptions → Plans*.

Then create a new plan.

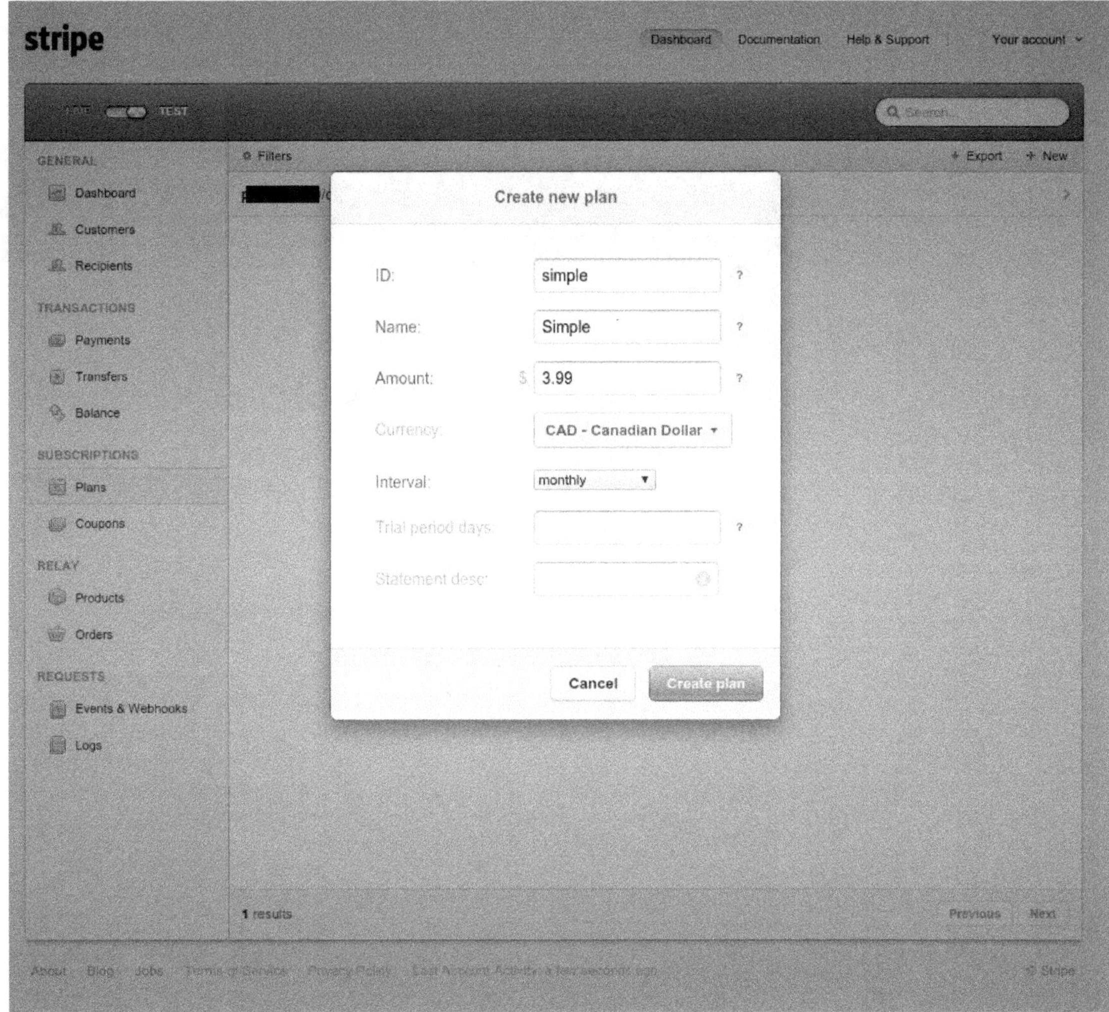


Where :

- **ID** is the billing tier identifier. It is **important** that this matches the ID of the billing tier in PacketFence.
- **Amount** is the price of the plan. It is **important** that this matches the price of the billing tier in PacketFence.
- **Currency** is the currency that will be used in the transactions. It is **important** that this matches the currency of the Stripe source in PacketFence.
- **Interval** is the interval at which the customer should be billed. In the case of this example, it is monthly.

Now, following the same procedure, create the advanced plan.

## Receiving updates from Stripe

As the subscription can be cancelled by a user, you need to setup your PacketFence installation to receive updates from Stripe.

Updates are sent using HTTP requests on a public IP.

You need to make sure that your PacketFence server is available through a public IP on port 80 and that your PacketFence server hostname resolves on the public domain.

Then, in Stripe, configure a *Webhook* so Stripe informs PacketFence of any event that happens in this Stripe merchant account.

In order to do so go in *Your Account → Account Settings → Webhooks* and click *Add endpoint*.

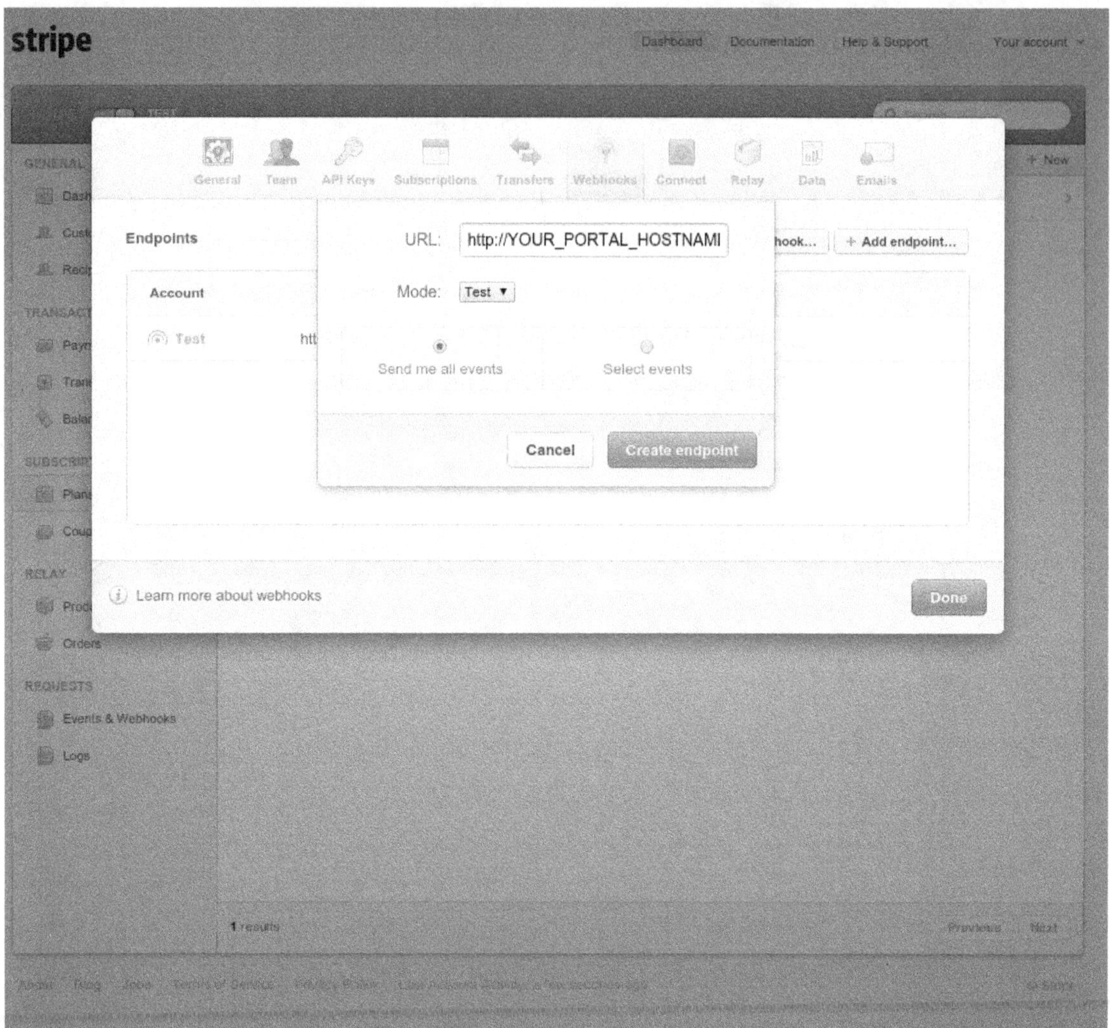


Where :

- **URL** is the URL to the PacketFence server. This should be http://YOUR_PORTAL_HOSTNAME/hook/billing/stripe
- **Mode** is whether this webhook is for testing mode or live mode

Now every time a user unsubscribes from a plan, PacketFence will be notified and will unregister that device from your network.

## Extending access before it ends

PacketFence allows users to extend their access before it has ended. In order to do so, you need to enable *Allow access to registration portal when registered* accessible via the *Captive Portal* tab of the *Connection Profiles*. Once this is activated, the users can reach https://YOUR_PORTAL_IP/status and select *Extend your access* in order to be able to access the billing section after they have registered.

# Devices Registration

Users have the possibility to register their devices (Microsoft XBOX/XBOX360, Nintendo DS/Wii, Sony PlayStation and so on) right from a special portal page. When accessing this page, users will be prompted to login as if they were registering themselves. Once logged in, the portal will ask them to enter the device MAC address that will then be matched against a predefined list of authorized MAC OUI. The device will be registered with the user's id and can be assigned into a specific category for easier management.

Here's how to configure the whole thing. The portal page can be accessed by the following URL: https://YOUR_PORTAL_HOSTNAME/device-registration This URL is accessible from within the network, in any VLAN that can reach the PacketFence server.

The following can be configured by editing the pf.conf file:

```
[registration]
device_registration = enabled
device_registration_role = gaming
```

Make sure the role exists in PacketFence otherwise you will encounter registration errors. Moreover, make sure the role mapping for your particular equipment is done.

These parameters can also be configured from the **Configuration → → Advanced Access Configuration → Device Registration** section.

Note

A *portal* interface type is required to use this feature. A *portal* interface type can be added to any network interface using the web admin GUI.

# Eduroam

> eduroam (education roaming) is the secure, world-wide roaming access service developed for the international research and education community.
>
> eduroam allows students, researchers and staff from participating institutions to obtain Internet connectivity across campus and when visiting other participating institutions by simply opening their laptop.
>
> — eduroam *https://www.eduroam.org/*

PacketFence supports integration with eduroam and allows participating institutions to authenticate both locally visiting users from other institutions as well as allowing other institutions to authenticate local users.

In order for PacketFence to allow eduroam authentication, the FreeRADIUS configuration of PacketFence must be modified to allow the eduroam servers to connect to it as clients as well as to proxy RADIUS authentication requests for users from outside institutions.

First, modify the /usr/local/pf/raddb/clients.conf file to allow the eduroam servers to connect to your PacketFence server. Add the eduroam servers as clients and make sure to add the proper RADIUS secret. Set a shortname to refer to these clients as you will later need it to exclude them from some parts of the PacketFence configuration.

clients.conf example:

```
client tlrs1.eduroam.us {
        secret = useStrongerSecret
        shortname = tlrs1
}

client tlrs2.eduroam.us {
        secret = useStrongerSecret
        shortname = tlrs2
}
```

Secondly, modify the list of domains and proxy servers in /usr/local/pf/raddb/proxy.conf. You will need to define each of your domains as well as the DEFAULT domain. The DEFAULT realm will apply to any client that attempts to authenticate with a realm that is not otherwise defined in proxy.conf and will be proxied to the eduroam servers.

Define one or more home servers (servers to which eduroam requests should be proxied).

proxy.conf example:

```
home_server tlrs1.eduroam.us {
        type = auth
        ipaddr = 257.128.1.1
        port = 1812
        secret = useStrongerSecret
        require_message_authenticator = yes
}
```

Define a pool of servers to group your eduroam home servers together.

proxy.conf example:

```
home_server_pool eduroam {
        type = fail-over
        home_server = tlrs1.eduroam.us
        home_server = tlrs2.eduroam.us
}
```

Define realms to select which requests should be proxied to the eduroam server pool. There should be one realm for each of your domains, and possibly one more per domain if you intend to allow usernames of the DOMAIN\user form.

The REALM is set based on the domain found by the suffix or ntdomain modules ( see raddb/modules/realm ). The suffix or ntdomain modules try to find a domain either with an @domain or suffix\username.

- If none is found, the REALM is NULL.
- If a domain is found, FreeRADIUS tries to match one of the REALMS defined in this file.
- If the domain is either example.edu or EXAMPLE FreeRADIUS sets the corresponding REALM, i.e. example.edu or EXAMPLE.
- If the REALM does not match either (and it isn't NULL), that means there was a domain other than EXAMPLE or example.edu and we assume it is meant to be proxied to eduroam. FreeRADIUS sets the DEFAULT realm (which is proxied to the eduroam authentication pool).

The REALM determines where the request is sent to. If the REALM authenticates locally the requests are processed entirely by FreeRADIUS. If the REALM sets a different home server pool, the requests are proxied to the servers defined within that pool.

proxy.conf example:

```
# This realm is for requests which don't have an explicit realm
# prefix or suffix.  User names like "bob" will match this one.
# No authentication server is defined, thus the authentication is
# done locally.
realm NULL {
}

# This realm is for ntdomain users who might use the domain like
# this "EXAMPLE\username".
# No authentication server is defined, thus the authentication is
# done locally.
realm EXAMPLE {
}

# This realm is for suffix users who use the domain like this:
# "username@example.edu".
# No authentication server is defined, thus the authentication is
# done locally.
realm example.edu {
}

# This realm is for ALL OTHER requests. Meaning in this context,
# eduroam. The auth_pool is set to the eduroam pool and so the
# requests will be proxied.
realm DEFAULT {
    auth_pool  = eduroam
    nostrip
}
```

Thirdly, you must configure the packetfence FreeRADIUS virtual servers to treat the requests properly.

In /usr/local/pf/raddb/sites-enabled/packetfence, modify the authorize section like this:

raddb/sites-enabled/packetfence example:

```
authorize {
        # pay attention to the order of the modules. It matters.
        ntdomain
        suffix
        preprocess

        # uncomment this section if you want to block eduroam users from
        # you other SSIDs. The attribute name ( Called-Station-Id ) may
        # differ based on your controller
        #if ( Called-Station-Id !~ /eduroam$/i) {
        #    update control {
        #        Proxy-To-Realm := local
        #    }
        #}

        eap {
                ok = return
        }


        files
        expiration
        logintime
        packetfence
}
```

In /usr/local/pf/raddb/sites-enabled/packetfence-tunnel, modify the post-auth section like this. If you omit this change the request will be sent to PacketFence where it will be failed since the eduroam servers are not part of your configured switches.

raddb/sites-enabled/packetfence-tunnel example:

```
post-auth {
        exec

        # we skip packetfence when the request is coming from the eduroam servers
        if ( "%{client:shortname}" != "tlrs1" && \
             "%{client:shortname}" != "tlrs2"    ) {
                packetfence
        }

        Post-Auth-Type REJECT {
                attr_filter.access_reject
        }
}
```

Finally, make sure that the realms module is configured this way ( see /usr/local/pf/raddb/modules/realm ):

raddb/modules/realm example:

```
# 'username@realm'
realm suffix {
        format = suffix
        delimiter = "@"
}

#  'domain\user'
realm ntdomain {
        format = prefix
        delimiter = "\\"
        ignore_null = yes
}
```

# Fingerbank integration

Fingerbank, a great device profiling tool developed alongside of PacketFence, now integrates with it to power-up the feature set allowing a PacketFence administrator to easily trigger violations based on different device types, device parents, DHCP fingerprints, DHCP vendor IDs, MAC vendors and browser user agents.

The core of that integration resides in the ability for a PacketFence system, to interact with the Fingerbank upstream project, which then allow a daily basis fingerprints database update, sharing unknown data so that more complex algorithms can process that new data to integrate it in the global database, querying the global upstream database in the case of an unknown match and much more.

Since the Fingerbank integration is now the "de facto" device profiling tool of PacketFence, it was a requirement to make it as simple as possible to configure and to use. From the moment a working PacketFence system is in place, Fingerbank is also ready to be used, but only in a "local" mode, which means, no interaction with the upstream Fingerbank project.

## Onboarding

To benefit from all the advantages of the Fingerbank project, the onboarding step is required to create an API key that will then allow interaction with the upstream project. That can easily be done only by going in the "Settings" menu item under the "Fingerbank" section of the PacketFence "Configuration" tab. From there, an easy process to create and save an user/organization specific API key can be followed. Once completed, the full feature set of Fingerbank can be used.

## Update Fingerbank database

Updating the Fingerbank data can't be easier. The only requirement is the onboarding process which allows you to interact with upstream project. Once done, an option to "Update Fingerbank DB" can be found on top of every menu item sections under "Fingerbank". Process may take a minute or two, depending on the size of the database and the internet connectivity, after which a success or error message will be show accordingly. "Local" records are NOT being modified during this process.

## Submit unknown data

Saying that we don't know everything is not false modesty. In that sense, the "Submit Unknown/ Unmatched Fingerprints" option is made available (after onboarding) so that unknown fingerprinting data going in and out on your network can easily be submitted to the upstream Fingerbank project for further analysis and integration the in the global database.

## Upstream interrogation

By default, PacketFence is configured to interrogate the upstream Fingerbank project (if onboarding has been completed) to fulfill a query with unmatched local results. Unmatched local results can result of an older version of the Fingerbank database or a requirement for a more complex algorithm due to the data set. That behavior is completely transparent and can be modified using the "Settings" menu item under the "Fingerbank"section of the PacketFence "Configuration" tab.

## Local entries

It is possible for an administrator who wants to customize an existing record (or create a new one) to do so using the "Local" entries. An upstream record (DHCP Fingerprint, DHCP Vendor, MAC Vendor, User Agent, Device type, even a Combination) can be cloned and then modified on a local basis if needed. Local records are always matched first since their purpose is to *override* an existing one. A local combination can be created to match either "Local" or "Upstream" or both entries to allow identification of a device.

## Settings

Fingerbank settings can easily be modified from the "Settings" menu item under the "Fingerbank" section of the PacketFence "Configuration" tab. There's documentation for each an every parameter that allow easier understanding.

# Floating Network Devices

Starting with version 1.9, PacketFence now supports floating network devices. A Floating network device is a device for which PacketFence has a different behavior compared to a regular device. This functionality was originally added to support mobile Access Points.

Caution

Right now PacketFence only supports floating network devices on Cisco and Nortel switches configured with port-security.

For a regular device, PacketFence put it in the VLAN corresponding to its status (Registration, Quarantine or Regular VLAN) and authorizes it on the port (port-security).

A floating network device is a device that PacketFence does not manage as a regular device.

When a floating network device is plugged, PacketFence will let/allow all the MAC addresses that will be connected to this device (or appear on the port) and if necessary, configure the port as multi-vlan (trunk) and set PVID and tagged VLANs on the port.

When an floating network device is unplugged, PacketFence will reconfigure the port like before it was plugged.

## How it works

Configuration:

- floating network devices have to be identified using their MAC address.
- linkup/linkdown traps are not enabled on the switches, only port-security traps are.

When PacketFence receives a port-security trap for a floating network device, it changes the port configuration so that:

- it disables port-security
- it sets the PVID
- it eventually sets the port as multi-vlan (trunk) and sets the tagged Vlans
- it enables linkdown traps

When PF receives a linkdown trap on a port in which a floating network device was plugged, it changes the port configuration so that:

- it enables port-security
- it disables linkdown traps

## Identification

As we mentioned earlier, each floating network device has to be identified. There are two ways to do it:

- by editing `conf/floating_network_device.conf`
- through the Web GUI, in **Configuration → Network Configuration → Floating Device**

Here are the settings that are available:

| | |
|---|---|
| MAC Address | MAC address of the floating device |
| IP Address | IP address of the floating device (not required, for information only) |
| trunkPort | Yes/no. Should the port be configured as a multi-vlan port? |
| pvid | VLAN in which PacketFence should put the port |
| taggedVlan | Comma separated list of VLANs. If the port is a multi-vlan, these are the Vlans that have to be tagged on the port. |

# OAuth2 Authentication

Note

OAuth2 authentication does not work with Webauth enforcement

The captive portal of PacketFence allows a guest/user to register using his Google, Facebook, LinkedIn, Windows Live, Twitter, Instagram, Pinterest or Github account.

For each providers, we maintain an allowed domain list to punch holes into the firewall so the user can hit the provider login page. This list is available in each OAuth2 authentication source.

You must enable the passthrough option in your PacketFence configuration (fencing.passthrough in pf.conf).

## Google

In order to use Google as a OAuth2 provider, you need to get an API key to access their services. Sign up here : http://code.google.com/apis/console. Make sure you use this URI for the "Redirect URI" field : https://YOUR_PORTAL_HOSTNAME/oauth2/callback. Of course, replace the hostname with the values from `general.hostname` and `general.domain`.

You can keep the default configuration, modify the App ID & App Secret (Given by Google on the developer platform) and Portal URL (https://YOUR_PORTAL_HOSTNAME/oauth2/callback).

Also, add the following Authorized domains : *.google.com, *.google.ca, *.google.fr, *.gstatic.com,googleapis.com,accounts.youtube.com (Make sure that you have the google domain from your country like Canada ⇒ *.google.ca, France ⇒ *.google.fr, etc...)

Once you have your client id, and API key, you need to configure the OAuth2 provider. This can be done by adding a Google OAuth2 authentication source from **Configuration → Policies and Access Control → Sources**.

Moreover, don't forget to add Google as a registration mode from your connection profile definition, available from **Configuration → Policies and Access Control → Connection Profiles and Pages**.

## Facebook

To use Facebook, you also need an API code and a secret key. To get one, go here: https://developers.facebook.com/apps. When you create your App, make sure you specify the following as the Website URL: https://YOUR_PORTAL_HOSTNAME/oauth2/callback

Of course, replace the hostname with the values from `general.hostname` and `general.domain`.

You can keep the default configuration, modify the App ID & App Secret (Given by Facebook on the developer platform) and Portal URL (https://YOUR_PORTAL_HOSTNAME/oauth2/callback).

Also, add the following Authorized domains : *.facebook.com, *.fbcdn.net, *.akamaihd.net (May change)

Once you have your information, you need to configure the OAuth2 provider. This can be done by adding a Facebook OAuth2 authentication source from **Configuration → Policies and Access Control → Sources**.

Moreover, don't forget to add Facebook as a registration mode from your connection profile definition, available from **Configuration → Policies and Access Control → Connection Profiles and Pages**.

Caution

By allowing OAuth through Facebook, you will give Facebook access to the users while they are sitting in the registration VLAN.

## Github

To use Github, you also need an API code and a secret key. To get one, you need to create an App here: https://github.com/settings/applications. When you create your App, make sure you specify the following as the Callback URL https://YOUR_PORTAL_HOSTNAME/oauth2/callback

Of course, replace the hostname with the values from `general.hostname` and `general.domain`.

Once you have your information, you need to configure the OAuth2 provider. This can be done by adding a GitHub OAuth2 authentication source from **Configuration → Policies and Access Control → Sources**.

Moreover, don't forget to add GitHub as a registration mode from your connection profile definition, available from **Configuration → Policies and Access Control → Connection Profiles and Pages**.

## Instagram

To use Instagram, you also need an API code and a secret key. To get one, go here: https://www.instagram.com/developer/clients/manage/. When you create your App, make sure you specify the following as the Website URL: https://YOUR_PORTAL_HOSTNAME/oauth2/callback

Of course, replace the hostname with the values from `general.hostname` and `general.domain`.

Once you have your information, you need to configure the OAuth2 provider. This can be done by adding a Instagram OAuth2 authentication source from **Configuration → Policies and Access Control → Sources**.

Moreover, don't forget to add Instagram as a registration mode from your connection profile definition, available from **Configuration → Policies and Access Control → Connection Profiles and Pages**.

## LinkedIn

To use LinkedIn, you also need an API code and a secret key. To get one, you need to create an App here: https://developer.linkedin.com/. When you create your App, make sure you specify the following as the Callback URL https://YOUR_PORTAL_HOSTNAME/oauth2/callback

Of course, replace the hostname with the values from `general.hostname` and `general.domain`.

Once you have your information, you need to configure the OAuth2 provider. This can be done by adding a LinkedIn OAuth2 authentication source from **Configuration → Policies and Access Control → Sources**.

Moreover, don't forget to add LinkedIn as a registration mode from your connection profile definition, available from **Configuration → Policies and Access Control → Connection Profiles and Pages**.

Also, LinkedIn requires a *state* parameter for the authorization URL. If you modify it, make sure to add it at the end of your URL.

## Pinterest

To use Pinterest, you also need an API code and a secret key. To get one, go here: https://developers.pinterest.com/apps. When you create your App, make sure you specify the following as the Redirect URL: https://YOUR_PORTAL_HOSTNAME/oauth2/callback

Of course, replace the hostname with the values from `general.hostname` and `general.domain`.

Once you have your information, you need to configure the OAuth2 provider. This can be done by adding a Pinterest OAuth2 authentication source from **Configuration → Policies and Access Control → Sources**.

Moreover, don't forget to add Pinterest as a registration mode from your connection profile definition, available from **Configuration → Policies and Access Control → Connection Profiles and Pages**.

## Twitter

To use Twitter, you also need an API code and a secret key which Twitter calls *consumer key* and *consumer secret*. Obtain this information by creating an new application from your Twitter Apps Management page. When you create your App, make sure you specify the following as the *Callback URL* https://YOUR_PORTAL_HOSTNAME/oauth2/callback

Of course, replace the hostname with the values from `general.hostname` and `general.domain`.

Once you have your information, you need to configure the OAuth2 provider. This can be done by adding a Twitter OAuth2 authentication source from **Configuration → Policies and Access Control → Sources**.

Moreover, don't forget to add Twitter as a registration mode from your connection profile definition, available from **Configuration → Policies and Access Control → Connection Profiles and Pages**.

## Windows Live

To use Windows live, you also need an API code and a secret key. To get one, you need to create an App here: https://account.live.com/developers/applications. When you create your App, make sure you specify the following as the Callback URL https://YOUR_PORTAL_HOSTNAME/oauth2/callback

Of course, replace the hostname with the values from `general.hostname` and `general.domain`.

Once you have your information, you need to configure the OAuth2 provider. This can be done by adding a WindowsLive OAuth2 authentication source from **Configuration → Policies and Access Control → Sources**.

Moreover, don't forget to add WindowsLive as a registration mode from your connection profile definition, available from **Configuration → Policies and Access Control → Connection Profiles and Pages**.

# Passthroughs

Passthroughs are used to allow access to certain resources that are outside of the registration VLAN for the users that are in it. A good example would be when you want to allow access to a password reset server even for clients that are currently on the captive portal.

There are two solutions for passthroughs - one using DNS resolution and iptables and the other one using Apache's mod_proxy module. Note that non-HTTP (including HTTPS) protocols cannot use the mod_proxy approach. You can use one of them or both but for if a domain is configured in both, DNS passthroughs have a higher priority.

In order to use the passthroughs feature in PacketFence, you need to enable it from the GUI in **Configuration→Network Configuration→Networks→Fencing**, enable **Passthrough** and then save.

## DNS passthroughs

If you just enabled the passthroughs, you should restart the iptables services after configuring the parameter (`/usr/local/pf/bin/pfcmd service iptables restart`).

Then add passthroughs in **Configuration→Network Configuration→Networks→Fencing→Passthroughs**. They can be of the following format:

- **example.com**: opens ports 80 and 443 in TCP for example.com
- **example.com:1812**: opens the port 1812 in TCP and UDP for example.com
- **example.com:tcp:1812**: opens the port 1812 in TCP for example.com
- **example.com:udp:1812**: opens the port 1812 in UDP for example.com

In addition to the options above, you can prefix the domain with `*.` (*.example.com) to white list all the subdomains of example.com (ex: `www.example.com`, `my.example.com`).

Should you combine multiple times the same domain with different ports (`example.com,example.com:udp:1812,example.com:udp:1813`) in the passthroughs, it will open all ports specified in all entries. In the previous example that would open ports 80, 443 in TCP as well as 1812 and 1813 in UDP.

Now when pfdns receives a request for one of these domains, it will reply with the real DNS records for the FQDN instead of a response that points to the captive portal. At the same time, it will add the entry to a special ipset which will allow access to the real IP address attached the FQDN via iptables based routing.

## mod_proxy passthroughs

The proxy passthroughs can be configured in **Configuration→Network Configuration→Networks→Fencing→Proxy Passthroughs**. Add a new FQDN (can also be a wildcard domain like *.google.com). Port specific passthroughs cannot be used as these only apply to port 80 in TCP. Then for this FQDN, pfdns will still answer with the IP address of the captive portal and when a device hits the captive portal, PacketFence will detect that this FQDN has a passthrough configured in PacketFence and will forward the traffic to mod_proxy.

# Production DHCP access

In order to perform all of its access control duties, PacketFence needs to be able to map MAC addresses into IP addresses.

For all the networks/VLANs where you want PacketFence to have the ability to isolate a node or to have IP information about nodes, you will need to perform **one** of the techniques below.

Also note that this doesn't need to be done for the registration, isolation VLANs and inline interfaces since PacketFence acts as the DHCP server in these networks.

## IP Helpers (recommended)

If you are already using IP Helpers for your production DHCP in your production VLANs this approach is the simplest one and the one that works the best.

Add PacketFence's management IP address as the last `ip helper-address` statement in your network equipment. At this point PacketFence will receive a copy of all DHCP requests for that VLAN and will record what IP were distributed to what node using a `pfdhcplistener` daemon.

By default no DHCP Server should be running on that interface where you are sending the requests. This is by design otherwise PacketFence would reply to the DHCP requests which would be a bad thing.

## Obtain a copy of the DHCP traffic

Get a copy of all the DHCP Traffic to a dedicated physical interface in the PacketFence server and run `pfdhcplistener` on that interface. It will involve configuring your switch properly to perform port mirroring (aka network span) and adding in PacketFence the proper interface statement at the operating system level and in `pf.conf`.

`/etc/sysconfig/network-scripts/ifcfg-eth2`:

```
DEVICE=eth2
ONBOOT=yes
BOOTPROTO=none
```

Add to `pf.conf`: (IPs are not important they are there only so that PacketFence will start)

```
[interface eth2]
mask=255.255.255.0
type=dhcp-listener
gateway=192.168.1.5
ip=192.168.1.1
```

Restart PacketFence and you should be good to go.

## Interface in every VLAN

Because DHCP traffic is broadcast traffic, an alternative for small networks with few local VLANs is to put a VLAN interface for every VLAN on the PacketFence server and have a `pfdhcplistener` listen on that VLAN interface.

On the network side you need to make sure that the VLAN truly reaches all the way from your client to your DHCP infrastructure up to the PacketFence server.

On the PacketFence side, first you need an operating system VLAN interface like the one below. Stored in `/etc/sysconfig/network-scripts/ifcfg-eth0.1010`:

```
# Engineering VLAN
DEVICE=eth0.1010
ONBOOT=yes
BOOTPROTO=static
IPADDR=10.0.101.4
NETMASK=255.255.255.0
VLAN=yes
```

Then you need to specify in `pf.conf` that you are interested in that VLAN's DHCP by setting type to `dhcp-listener`.

```
[interface eth0.1010]
mask=255.255.255.0
type=dhcp-listener
gateway=10.0.101.1
ip=10.0.101.4
```

Repeat the above for all your production VLANs then restart PacketFence.

## Host production DHCP on PacketFence

It's an option. Just modify `conf/dhcpd.conf` so that it will host your production DHCP properly and make sure that a `pfdhcplistener` runs on the same interface where production DHCP runs. However, please note that this is **NOT** recommended. See this ticket to see why.

# Proxy Interception

PacketFence enables you to intercept proxy requests and forward them to the captive portal. It only works one layer-2 networks because PacketFence must be the default gateway. In order to use the Proxy Interception feature, you need to enable it from the GUI in **Configuration → Network Configuration → Networks → Fencing** and check **Proxy Interception**.

Add the port you want to intercept (like 8080 or 3128) and add a new entry in the `/etc/hosts` file to resolve the fully qualified domain name (fqdn) of the captive portal to the IP address of the registration interface. This modification is mandatory in order for Apache to receives the proxy requests.

# Routed Networks

If your isolation and registration networks are not locally-reachable (at layer 2) on the network, but routed to the PacketFence server, you'll have to let the PacketFence server know this. PacketFence can even provide DHCP and DNS in these routed networks and provides an easy to use configuration interface.

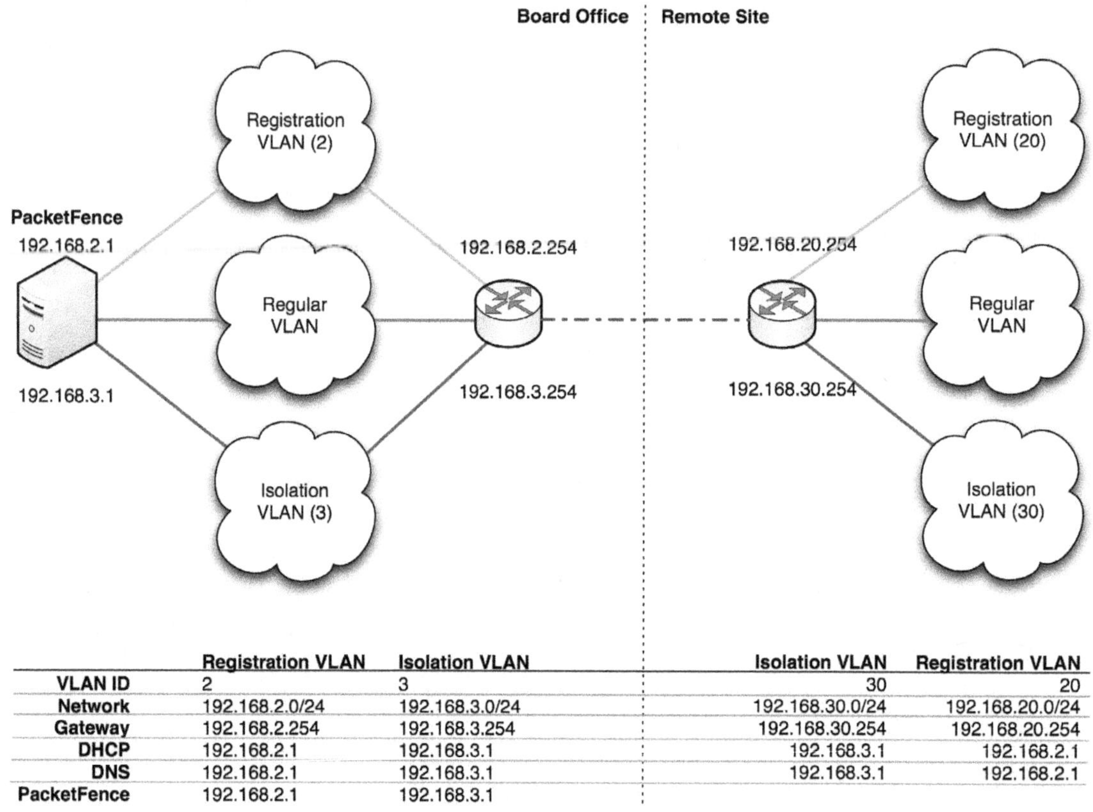


| | Registration VLAN | Isolation VLAN | Isolation VLAN | Registration VLAN |
|---|---|---|---|---|
| VLAN ID | 2 | 3 | 30 | 20 |
| Network | 192.168.2.0/24 | 192.168.3.0/24 | 192.168.30.0/24 | 192.168.20.0/24 |
| Gateway | 192.168.2.254 | 192.168.3.254 | 192.168.30.254 | 192.168.20.254 |
| DHCP | 192.168.2.1 | 192.168.3.1 | 192.168.3.1 | 192.168.2.1 |
| DNS | 192.168.2.1 | 192.168.3.1 | 192.168.3.1 | 192.168.2.1 |
| PacketFence | 192.168.2.1 | 192.168.3.1 | | |

For dhcpd, make sure that the clients DHCP requests are correctly forwarded (IP Helpers in the remote routers) to the PacketFence server. Then make sure you followed the instructions in the DHCP and DNS Server Configuration (networks.conf) for your locally accessible network.

If we consider the network architecture illustrated in the above schema, **conf/pf.conf** will include the local registration and isolation interfaces only.

```
[interface eth0.2]
enforcement=vlan
ip=192.168.2.1
type=internal
mask=255.255.255.0
```

```
[interface eth0.3]
enforcement=vlan
ip=192.168.3.1
type=internal
mask=255.255.255.0
```

### Note

PacketFence will not start unless you have at least one *internal* interface, so you need to create local registration and isolation VLANs even if you don't intend to use them. Also, the *internal* interfaces are the only ones on which dhcpd listens, so the remote registration and isolation subnets need to point their DHCP helper-address to those particular IPs.

Then you need to provide the routed networks information to PacketFence. You can do it through the GUI in **Administration → Networks** (or in `conf/networks.conf`).

`conf/networks.conf` will look like this:

```
[192.168.2.0]
netmask=255.255.255.0
gateway=192.168.2.1
next_hop=
domain-name=registration.example.com
dns=192.168.2.1
dhcp_start=192.168.2.10
dhcp_end=192.168.2.200
dhcp_default_lease_time=300
dhcp_max_lease_time=600
type=vlan-registration
named=enabled
dhcpd=enabled
```

```
[192.168.3.0]
netmask=255.255.255.0
gateway=192.168.3.1
next_hop=
domain-name=isolation.example.com
dns=192.168.3.1
dhcp_start=192.168.3.10
dhcp_end=192.168.3.200
dhcp_default_lease_time=300
dhcp_max_lease_time=600
type=vlan-isolation
named=enabled
dhcpd=enabled
```

```
[192.168.20.0]
netmask=255.255.255.0
gateway=192.168.20.254
next_hop=192.168.2.254
domain-name=registration.example.com
dns=192.168.2.1
dhcp_start=192.168.20.10
dhcp_end=192.168.20.200
dhcp_default_lease_time=300
dhcp_max_lease_time=600
type=vlan-registration
named=enabled
dhcpd=enabled
```

```
[192.168.30.0]
netmask=255.255.255.0
gateway=192.168.30.254
next_hop=192.168.3.254
domain-name=isolation.example.com
dns=192.168.3.1
dhcp_start=192.168.30.10
dhcp_end=192.168.30.200
dhcp_default_lease_time=300
dhcp_max_lease_time=600
type=vlan-isolation
named=enabled
dhcpd=enabled
```

DHCP clients on the registration and isolation networks receive the PF server IP as their DNS server (dns=x.x.x.x), and PF spoofs DNS responses to force clients via the portal. However, clients could manually configure their DNS settings to escape the portal. To prevent this you will need to apply an ACL on the access router nearest the clients, permitting access only to the PF server and local DHCP broadcast traffic.

For example, for the VLAN 20 remote registration network:

```
ip access-list extended PF_REGISTRATION
 permit ip any host 192.168.2.1
 permit udp any any eq 67
 deny ip any any log
interface vlan 20
 ip address 192.168.20.254 255.255.255.0
 ip helper-address 192.168.2.1
 ip access-group PF_REGISTRATION in
```

If your edge switches support *vlan-isolation* you can also apply the ACL there. This has the advantage of preventing machines in isolation from attempting to attack each other.

# VLAN Filter Definition

We added the ability to specify filters directly in the portion of code that re-evaluates the VLAN or do a call to the API.

These rules are available in different scopes:

```
ViolationRole
RegistrationRole
RegisteredRole
InlineRole
AutoRegister
NodeInfoForAutoReg
```

And can be defined using different criteria like:

```
node_info.attribute (like node_info.status)
switch
ifIndex
mac
connection_type
username
ssid
time
owner.attribute (like owner.pid)
radius_request.attribute (like radius_request.Calling-Station-Id)
```

For example, lets define a rule that prevents a device from connecting when its category is the "default", when the SSID is "SECURE" and when the current time is between 11am and 2pm: from Monday to Friday when it try to connect as a registered device :

```
[category]
filter = node_info.category
operator = is
value = default
```

```
[ssid]
filter = ssid
operator = is
value = SECURE
```

```
[time]
filter = time
operator = is
value = wd {Mon Tue Wed Thu Fri} hr {11am-2pm}
```

```
[1:category&ssid&time]
scope = RegisteredRole
role = nointernet
```

The second example will create a violation if the SSID is OPEN and the owner is igmout

```
[igmout]
filter = owner.pid
operator = is
value = igmout
```

```
[open]
filter = ssid
operator = is
value = OPEN
```

```
[2:igmout&ssid]
scope = RegisteredRole
action = trigger_violation
action_param = mac = $mac, tid = 1100012, type = INTERNAL
```

The third example will autoregister the device and assign the role staff to each device where the username is igmout.

```
[igmout]
filter = username
operator = is
value = igmout
```

```
[secure]
filter = ssid
operator = is
value = SECURE
```

```
[3:igmout&secure]
scope = AutoRegister
role = staff
```

```
[4:igmout&secure]
scope = NodeInfoForAutoReg
role = staff
```

You can have a look in the file vlan_filters.conf, there are some examples on how to use and define filters.

# RADIUS Filter Definition

We added the ability to specify filters directly in the portion of code that return the radius answer or do a call to the API.

These rules are only available in one scope:

```
returnRadiusAccessAccept
```

And can be defined using different criteria like:

```
node_info.attribute (like node_info.$attribute)
switch
ifIndex
mac
connection_type
username
ssid
time
owner.attribute (like owner.$attribute)
radius_request.attribute (like radius_request.$attribute)
violation
user_role
vlan
```

For example, lets define a rule that return Access Accept when the connection is Ethernet-EAP and when there is no violation (merge_return means that the original answer of PacketFence will be merge with the filter answer automatically):

```
[violation]
filter = violation
operator = defined
```

```
[etherneteap]
filter = connection_type
operator = is
value = Ethernet-EAP
```

```
[1:etherneteap&!violation]
merge_answer = no
scope = returnRadiusAccessAccept
```

In this other example we just add a new attribute to the original answer in the same conditions (here $user_role will be replaced by the real user role of the device and ${switch._portalURL} will be replaced by the value of _portalURL defined in the switch config):

```
[1:etherneteap&!violation]
merge_answer = yes
scope = returnRadiusAccessAccept
answer1 = Cisco-AVPair => url-redirect-acl=$user_role;url-redirect=
${switch._portalURL}/cep$session_id
```

You can have a look in the file radius_filters.conf, there are some examples on how to use and define filters.

# DNS enforcement

DNS enforcement allows you to control the network access of the device by using the pfdns service on PacketFence.

The architecture of DNS enforcement is as following : - DHCP and DNS are provided by the PacketFence server - The PacketFence DHCP server will provide the IP of your network equipment as the gateway and the IP address of the PacketFence DNS server to resolve names. - Routing is provided by another equipment on your network (Core switch, Firewall, Router,...) - If a user should be shown the portal, the pfdns service will return a pointer to the IP address of the captive portal, otherwise pfdns will resolve the name externally and use it in the reply.

This enforcement mode used by itself can be bypassed by the device by using a different DNS server or by using its own DNS cache.

The first can be prevented using an ACL on your routing equipment, the second can be prevented by combining DNS enforcement with Single-Sign-On on your network equipment. Please see the Firewall Single-Sign-On documentation for details on how to accomplish this.

In order to configure DNS enforcement, you first need to go in *Configuration → Network Configuration → Networks → Interfaces* then select one of your interfaces and set it in DNS enforcement mode.

After, you need to configure a routed network for this interface by clicking *Add routed network*. See the *Routed Networks* section of this document for details on how to configure it.

Note

If you are not using a routed network, you need to use Inline enforcement as DNS enforcement can only be used for routed networks.

Once this is done, you need to restart the dhcpd and pfdns services.

# Parked devices

In the event that you are managing a large registration network with devices that stay there (ex: Students that can't register in your environment), these devices consume precious resources and generate useless load on the captive portal and registration DHCP server.

Using the parking feature, you can make these devices have a longer lease and hit an extremely lightweight captive portal so that the amount of resources they consume is minimal. In that captive portal, they will see a message explaining that they haven't registered their device for a certain amount of time, and will let them leave the **parked** state by pressing a link.

The **parked** vs **unparked** state is controlled through violation `1300003` which gets triggered according to the `parking.threshold` setting (*Configuration→Network Configuration→Networks→Device Parking*).

So, in order to activate the parking, go in *Configuration→Network Configuration→Networks→Device Parking* and set the threshold to a certain amount of seconds. A suggested value would be `21600` which is 6 hours. This means that if a device stays in your registration network for more than 6 hours in a row, it will trigger violation `1300003` and place that device into the **parked** state.

In that same section, you can define the lease length of the user when he is in the **parked** state.

### Note

Parking is detected when a device asks for DHCP, if PacketFence is not your DHCP server for the registration network, this feature will not work. Also, if the device goes into the parked state with a lease time of 1 hour and the user immediately releases himself from the parking state, it will take 1 hour before the next detection takes place even if you set `parking.threshold` to a lower value.

## Violation 1300003

This violation controls what happens when a user is detected doing parking.

Here are the main settings:

- You can add actions to the predefined ones (like *Email admin* or *External action*) in *Definition → Actions*
- The amount of time a user can **unpark** their device is controlled through the *Remediation → Max enable* setting.
- The amount of grace time between two parking violations is controlled by the *Remediation → Grace* setting. This means, once a user release himself from the **parked** state, he will have at least this amount of time to register before the parking triggers again.
- The destination role (thus VLAN) of the user is controlled by *Advanced → Role*. You should leave the user in the registration role, but should you want to dedicate a role for parking, you can set it there.

- The **Template** attribute will only be used when the user is on the normal PacketFence portal and not the one dedicated for parking. If you want the user to access the non-parking portal, disable *Show parking portal* in *Configuration → Network Configuration → Networks → Device Parking*

# Custom reports

Using the `report.conf` configuration file, you can define reports that create SQL queries to view tables in the PacketFence database. These reports will appear under the *Reports* tab of the administration interface.

In order to configure a report, you need to edit `/usr/local/pf/conf/report.conf` and add a section that will define your report.

The following attributes are available to define your report (the ones that have an asterisk are mandatory):

- * `description` : The user friendly description that will display for this report
- * `base_table` : The base SQL table that will be used to create the view
- * `columns` : The columns to select from the table(s) (ex: `node.mac`).
- * `date_field` : The field to use for date filtering. Will also be used as default sorting field unless `order_fields` is set in the report.
- `joins` : The tables to join to the base table and how to join them. See example below and the following documentation.
- `group_field` : The field to group the entries by. No grouping is done if this field is omitted or empty.
- `order_fields` : Comma delimited fields for the ordering of the report. The field should be prefixed of `-` if the sort should be made in descending order for the field (ex: `-node.regdate,locationlog.start_time,+iplog.start_time`).
- `base_conditions` : Comma delimited conditions that should be applied to the report. This can be used to filter the report without using the search in the administration interface to provide the proper unsearched view. Conditions should match the following format : `field:operator:value` (ex: `auth_log.source:=:sms,auth_log.status:!=:completed`).
- `base_conditions_operator` : Whether the base conditions should be matched using an all or any logic. Accepted values are `all` and `any`.
- `searches` : Comma delimited searches that should be available on the report. Should match the following format `type:Display Name:field` (ex: `string:Username:auth_log.pid`).
  - `type` defines the type of the search, the only one currently supported is `string`.
  - `Display Name` is the user friendly name of the field for display.
  - `field` is the SQL name of the field to search

## Note

You should always prefix the fields with the table name and a dot (ex: `node.mac`, `locationlog.role`, ...) so that they are not ambiguous. Although your query may work with a single table, it will not if you decide to add joins that contain column name(s) that are the same as the base table.

## Examples:

View of the auth_log table:

```
[auth_log]
description=Authentication report
# The table to search from
base_table=auth_log
# The columns to select
columns=auth_log.*
# The date field that should be used for date ranges
date_field=attempted_at
# Allow searching on the PID displayed as Username
searches=string:Username:auth_log.pid
```

In this simple example, you will be able to select the whole content of the **auth_log** table and use the date range on the **attempted_at** field as well as search on the **pid** field when viewing the report.

View of the opened violations:

```
[open_violations]
description=Open violations
# The table to search from
base_table=violation
# The columns to select
columns=violation.vid as "Violation ID", violation.mac as "MAC Address",
 class.description as "Violation description", node.computername as "Hostname",
 node.pid as "Username", node.notes as "Notes", locationlog.switch_ip as "Last
 switch IP", violation.start_date as "Opened on"
# Left join node, locationlog on the MAC address and class on the violation ID
joins=<<EOT
=>{violation.mac=node.mac} node|node
=>{violation.mac=locationlog.mac} locationlog|locationlog
=>{violation.vid=class.vid} class|class
EOT
date_field=start_date
# filter on open locationlog entries or null locationlog entries via the end_date
 field
base_conditions_operator=any
base_conditions=locationlog.end_time:=:0000-00-00,locationlog.end_time:IS:
```

In the example above, you can see that the violation table is *left joined* to the class, node and locationlog tables. Using that strategy we make sure all the violations are listed even on deleted nodes. Then, base conditions are added to filter out outdated locationlog entries as well as include devices without locationlog entries. Removing those conditions would lead to duplicate entries being shown since the report would reflect all the historical locationlog entries.

# Admin Access

You can manage which access you give to PacketFence administrators. To do that go through *Configuration→System Configuration→Admin Access*. Then go to your source which authenticate administrator and create an *administration* rule and assign the wanted Admin role. This functionality allows you to have a granular control on which section of the admin interface is available to whom.

# Regex Syslog Parser

You are now able to create syslog parser using regex. This will allow you complex filters and rules to work on data receive via syslog.

Configuring a Regex Syslog Parser

- Enabled - You can enable/disable the parser from running
- Alert Pipe - A previously created alert pipe (FIFO)
- Rules - The list of rules that defines how to match log file entries and what action(s) to take when matching

Regex Syslog Parser Rule

- Name - The name of the rule
- Regex - The regex to match against a log entry. The regex may have named captures which can be used for parameter replacement start a $.
- Actions - A list of actions to take when the regex matches
- IP to MAC - Perform automatic translation of IPs to MACs and the other way around
- Last if matches - Stop processing the other rules if this rule matched

Defining Actions

An action have two parts

- method - The name of the action you want to take
- parameter list - The list of parameters you want to provide to the method. Each parameter is seperated by a comma. The parameters that are to be replaced by a named capture.

Example Action

Regex -

```
mac\s*:\s*(?&lt;mac&gt;[a-zA-Z0-9]{2}(:[a-zA-Z0-9]{2}){5}), notes\s*:\s*(?
&lt;notes&gt;.*)
```

Action -

```
modify_node:  mac, $mac, notes, $notes
```

Chapter 13

# Suricata example:

PacketFence already contains a syslog parser for Suricata. This is an example to raise a violation from a syslog alert on the Suricata SID.

The first step is to create the syslog regex parser and then create the violation.

# Syslog regex parser configuration:

To create the syslog regex parser you will need to go to **Configuration → Compliance → Syslog Parsers → Add a Syslog Parser → regex**

Here is the configuration of the syslog regex parser:

```
Detector *: Suricata
Enabled: checked
Alert pipe: /usr/local/pf/var/suricata (To create the fifo file, do: mkfifo /usr/
local/pf/var/suricata)
```

```
Rules:
```

```
Rule - New:
```

```
Name *: ET P2P Kaaza Media desktop p2pnetworking.exe
Regex *: (?<date>\d{2}\/\d{2}\/\d{4}-\d{2}:\d{2}:\d{2}.*?)  \[\*\*\] \[\d+:(?
<sid>\d+):\d+\] (?<message>.*?) \[\*\*\].* (?<srcip>\d{1,3}(\.\d{1,3}){3}):(?
<srcport>\d+) -> (?<ip>\d{1,3}(\.\d{1,3}){3}):(?<port>\d+)
Action: trigger_violation mac, $mac, tid, $sid, type, detect
Last if match: unchecked
IP to MAC: checked
```

Save the regex rule.

You can directly test your rule. In the previous example the parser expect a syslog string like this:

```
02/26/2017-14:29:00.524309  [**] [1:2000340:10] ET P2P Kaaza Media desktop
 p2pnetworking.exe Activity [**] [Classification: Potential Corporate Privacy
 Violation] [Priority: 1] {UDP} 173.194.7.75:443 -> 1.2.3.4:46742
```

In order to have a correct match in the rule, you will need to have a valid iplog entry in the database. Put the string in the test box and then click on the *RUN TEST* button, you should get:

```
Click to see actions for - 02/26/2017-14:29:00.524309 [**] [1:2000340:10]
 ET P2P Kaaza Media desktop p2pnetworking.exe Activity [**] [Classification:
 Potential Corporate Privacy Violation] [Priority: 1] {UDP} 173.194.7.75:443 ->
 1.2.3.4:46742
```

- ET P2P Kaaza Media desktop p2pnetworking.exe : trigger_violation(*mac*, *00:11:22:33:44:55*, *tid*, *2000340*, *type*, *detect*)

We can see that PacketFence will execute the violation on the MAC address 00:11:22:33:44:55.

# Violation creation:

Now you will need to create the violation with the trigger id *2000340* in order to isolate the device. In order to do so, go to **Configuration → Compliance → Violation → ADD VIOLATION**

Definition:

```
Enabled: ON
Identifier: 1500001
Description: ET P2P Kaaza Media
Action: Reevaluate Access Action; Log message
Priority: 1
```

Triggers:

- Click on the + button
- Look for *detect* in the dropdown list
- Add the trigger ID: 2000340 and click the ADD button
- Click on the < button next to *Select Some Options*

Remediation:

```
Auto Enable: checked
Max Enables: 2
Grace: 5 minutes
Template: p2p.html
```

Click on the SAVE button.

Now you will need to restart the pfqueue and the pfdetect services.

```
/usr/local/pf/bin/pfcmd service pfqueue restart
```

```
/usr/local/pf/bin/pfcmd service pfdetect restart
```

Make sure that you have your pipe file otherwise the process won't start.

Chapter 16

# StreamScan example:

This is an example to raise a violation from a syslog alert on a StreamScan alert ID.

The first step is to create the syslog regex parser and then create the violation.

# Syslog regex parser configuration:

To create the syslog regex parser you will need to go to **Configuration → Compliance → Syslog Parsers → Add a Syslog Parser → regex**

Here is the configuration of the syslog regex parser:

```
Detector *: StreamScan
Enabled: checked
Alert pipe: /usr/local/pf/var/streamscan (To create the fifo file, do: mkfifo /
usr/local/pf/var/streamscan)
```

```
Rules:
```

```
Rule - New:
```

```
Name *: SSH Alert
Regex *: CDS\[(?<cds_id>\d+)\].*device=(?<device_ip>\d+(\.\d+){3}) threat="(?
<threat>.*?)" direction=(?<direction>[^ ]+) sourceip=(?<sourceip>\d+(\.\d+)
{3}) sourceport=(?<sourceport>\d+) destip=(?<destip>\d+(\.\d+){3}) destport=(?
<destport>\d+) app=(?<app>[^ ]*) timestamp=(?<timestamp>[^ ]*) sid=(?<sid>[^ ]*)
Action: trigger_violation mac, $mac, tid, $sid, type, detect
Last if match: unchecked
IP to MAC: checked
```

Save the regex rule.

You can directly test your rule. In the previous example the parser expect a syslog string like this:

```
Apr  6 10:16:18 ubuntu CDS[83162]:type=violation device=172.20.20.193 threat="ssh
 trafic detected" direction=inbound sourceip=172.145.25.10 sourceport=22
 destip=172.145.25.10 destport=42290 app=ssh timestamp=2017-04-06_10-16-18.965687
 sid=1234
```

In order to have a correct match in the rule, you will need to have a valid iplog entry in the database. Put the string in the test box and then click on the *RUN TEST* button, you should get:

```
Results
```

```
Click to see actions for - Apr 6 10:16:18 ubuntu CDS[83162]:type=violation
 device=172.20.20.193 threat="ssh trafic detected" direction=inbound
 sourceip=172.145.25.10 sourceport=22 destip=172.145.25.10 destport=42290 app=ssh
 timestamp=2017-04-06_10-16-18.965687 sid=1234
- violation : trigger_violation('mac', '00:11:22:33:44:55', 'tid', '1234',
 'type', 'detect')
```

We can see that PacketFence will execute the violation on the MAC address 00:11:22:33:44:55.

# Violation creation:

Now you will need to create the violation with the trigger id *2000340* in order to isolate the device. In order to do so, go to **Configuration → Compliance → Violation → ADD VIOLATION**

Definition:

```
Enabled: ON
Identifier: 1234
Description: Illegal SSH traffic
Action: Reevaluate Access Action; Log message
Priority: 1
```

Triggers:

- Click on the + button
- Look for *detect* in the dropdown list
- Add the trigger ID: 2000340 and click the ADD button
- Click on the < button next to *Select Some Options*

Remediation:

```
Auto Enable: checked
Max Enables: 2
Grace: 5 minutes
Template: generic.html
```

Click on the SAVE button.

Now you will need to restart the pfqueue and the pfdetect services.

```
/usr/local/pf/bin/pfcmd service pfqueue restart
```

```
/usr/local/pf/bin/pfcmd service pfdetect restart
```

Make sure that you have your pipe file otherwise the process won't start.

# Optional components

## Blocking malicious activities with violations

Policy violations allow you to restrict client system access based on violations of certain policies. For example, if you do not allow P2P type traffic on your network, and you are running the appropriate software to detect it and trigger a violation for a given client, PacketFence will give that client a "blocked" page which can be customized to your wishes.

In order to be able to block malicious activities, installation and configuration of a PacketFence compatible IDS is required. PacketFence currently support Snort, Suricata and Security Onion.

### Suricata

#### Installation

Since the suricata IDS is not packaged with the distros (except maybe Fedora, which we do not officially support), you need to build it the "old" way.

The OISF provides a really well written how-to for that. It's available here: https://redmine.openinfosecfoundation.org/projects/suricata/wiki/CentOS5

Note

To benefit the OPSWAT Metadefender Cloud integration, Suricata needs to be built with libnss / libnspr support. Make sure to use JSON output. More information on how to achieve this can be found there: https://redmine.openinfosecfoundation.org/projects/suricata/wiki/MD5

#### Configuration

Depending on whether or not Suricata is running on the PacketFence server, configuration is different.

When running locally, PacketFence provides a basic `suricata.yaml` that can be modified to suit different needs. The file is located in `/usr/local/pf/conf`.

In the case that Suricata is running on a separate server, Suricata configuration will have to be handled separately, which is not the purpose of the present guide.

## OPSWAT Metadefender Cloud

It is possible to trigger violations based on threat level of downloaded files using the Metadefender Cloud integration in conjunction with the Suricata MD5 extraction feature. Without entering in the details, here are the basic steps to make it work.

First, an OPSWAT portal account is required to make use of the API. Such account can be obtained through the OPSWAT portal: https://portal.opswat.com.

Other requirement is a Suricata working installation built with libnss / libnspr support as described in the upper "Installation" section.

Along with the OPSWAT API key for Metadefender Cloud (they call it *License Key*) and the working Suricata installation, some configuration (PacketFence based AND Suricata based) is also required.

Assuming that all the steps for Suricata MD5 extraction have been followed, here's what to do next.

On PacketFence, under Configuration→Compliance→OPSWAT Metadefender, enter your *Licence Key*.

On the Suricata server (syslog-ng is preferred due to easier and more powerful configuration. If not installed, it might be an idea):

Configure `/etc/syslog-ng/syslog-ng.conf` by adding the following to enable sending MD5 file store log entries to PacketFence:

```
### PacketFence / OPSWAT Metadefender Cloud integration
# This line specifies where the files-json.log file is located
# -> Make sure to configure the right path along with the right filename
source s_suricata_files { file("/MY_SURICATA_LOG_FILES_PATH/files-json.log"
 program_override("suricata_files") flags(no-parse)); };
# This line tells syslog-ng to send the data read to the PacketFence management
 interface IP address using UDP 514
# -> Make sure to configure the right PacketFence management interface IP address
destination d_packetfence_md5 { udp("PACKETFENCE_MGMT_IP" port(514)); };
# This line indicates syslog-ng to use the s_suricata_files source and send it to
 the d_packetfence_md5 destination
log { source(s_suricata_files); destination(d_packetfence_md5); };
```

A restart of the syslog-ng daemon is required

```
service syslog-ng restart
```

On the PacketFence server:

Modify rsyslog configuration to allow incoming UDP packets by uncommenting the following two lines in `/etc/rsyslog.conf`:

```
$ModLoad imudp
$UDPServerRun 514
```

Configure `/etc/rsyslog.d/suricata_files.conf` so it contains the following which will redirect Suricata MD5 file store log entries and stop further processing of current matched message:

```
if $programname == 'suricata_files' then /usr/local/pf/var/suricata_files
& ~
```

Make sure the receiving alert pipe (FIFO) exists

```
mkfifo /usr/local/pf/var/suricata_files
```

Restart the rsyslog daemon

```
service rsyslog restart
```

At this point, Suricata should be able to extract MD5 checksum of downloaded files and send the related log entry to PacketFence.

A configuration of a new *syslog parser* as well as some violations are the only remaining steps to make full usage of the OPSWAT Metadefender Cloud integration.

Configuration of a new *syslog parser* (Configuration→Compliance→Syslog Parsers) should use the followings:

```
Type: suricata_md5
Alert pipe: the previously created alert pipe (FIFO) which is, in this case, /
usr/local/pf/var/suricata_files
```

Configuration of a new violation can use the following trigger types:

```
Type: metadefender
Triggers ID: The scan result returned by Metadefender Cloud online
```

```
Type: suricata_md5
Trigger ID: The MD5 hash returned by Suricata
```

# Security Onion

## Installation and Configuration

Security Onion is a Ubuntu based security suite. The latest installation instructions are available directly from the Security Onion website, https://github.com/Security-Onion-Solutions/security-onion/wiki/Installation

Since a security suite consists of multiple pieces of software tied together, you may be prompted for different options during the installation process. A detailed "Production Deployment" guide can also be found directly from the Security Onion website: https://github.com/Security-Onion-Solutions/security-onion/wiki/ProductionDeployment

## PacketFence integration

Once Security Onion is installed and minimally configured, integration with PacketFence is required to be able to raise violations based on sensor(s) alerts. syslog is used to forward sensor(s) alerts from Security Onion to the PacketFence detection mechanisms.

The simplest way is as follow (based on https://github.com/Security-Onion-Solutions/security-onion/wiki/ThirdPartyIntegration);

On the Security Onion server:

Note

Must be done on the master server running *sguild*.

Configure `/etc/syslog-ng/syslog-ng.conf` by adding the following to enable sending sguild log entries to PacketFence:

```
### PacketFence / IDS integration
# This line specifies where the sguild.log file is located
# -> Make sure to configure the right path along with the right filename (on a
 Security Onion setup, that should be pretty much standard)
source s_sguil { file("/var/log/nsm/securityonion/sguild.log"
 program_override("securityonion_ids")); };
# This line filters on the string "Alert Received"
filter f_sguil { match("Alert Received"); };
# This line tells syslog-ng to send the data read to the PacketFence management
 IP address using UDP 514
# -> Make sure to configure the right PacketFence management interface IP address
destination d_packetfence_alerts { udp("PACKETFENCE_MGMT_IP" port(514)); };
# This line indicates syslog-ng to use the s_sguil source, apply the f_sguil
 filter and send it to the d_packetfence_alerts destination
log { source(s_sguil); filter(f_sguil); destination(d_packetfence_alerts); };
```

Sending sguild alert output to syslog requires DEBUG to be changed from 1 to 2 under `/etc/sguild/sguild.conf`

```
set DEBUG 2
```

A restart of the sguild daemon is then required

```
sudo nsm_server_ps-restart
```

A restart of the syslog-ng daemon is then required

```
service syslog-ng restart
```

On the PacketFence server:

Modify rsyslog configuration to allow incoming UDP packets by uncommenting the following two lines in `/etc/rsyslog.conf`:

```
$ModLoad imudp
$UDPServerRun 514
```

Configure `/etc/rsyslog.d/securityonion_ids.conf` so it contains the following which will redirect Security Onion sguild log entries and stop further processing of current matched message:

```
if $programname == 'securityonion_ids' then /usr/local/pf/var/securityonion_ids
& ~
```

Make sure the receiving alert pipe (FIFO) exists

```
mkfifo /usr/local/pf/var/securityonion_ids
```

Restart the rsyslog daemon

```
service rsyslog restart
```

At this point, Security Onion should be able to send detected alerts log entries to PacketFence.

A configuration of a new *syslog parser* as well as some violations are the only remaining steps to make full usage of the Security Onion IDS integration.

Configuration of a new *syslog parser* should use the followings:

```
Type: security_onion
Alert pipe: the previously created alert pipe (FIFO) which is, in this case, /
usr/local/pf/var/securityonion_ids
```

Configuration of a new violation can use the following trigger types:

```
Type: detect
Triggers ID: The IDS triggered rule ID
```

```
Type: suricata_event
Trigger ID: The rule class of the triggered IDS alert
```

## ERSPAN

ERSPAN permits to mirror a local port traffic (low bandwidth) to a remote IP, E.G: your Security Onion already deployed box. ERSPAN encapsulates port traffic into ERSPAN then GRE and send that traffic to one/multiple destination(s). ERSPAN is a Cisco technology which is available only on some platforms, including: Catalyst 6500, 7600, Nexus, and ASR 1000.

One way of accessing encapsulated traffic at the destination host is through a software called RCDCAP, which is a daemon that creates a virtual interface if not existing, on which both GRE and ERSPAN headers are decapsulated prior to the traffic being injected to the previous interface. Security Onion can then feed on that interface like it would on any other, and if the RCDCAP daemon dies, continue to listen to that interface even though decapsulated traffic won't be available anymore.

Assumptions for the example: The switch is at IP 172.16.0.1, the monitored switch port is GigabitEthernet0/10 and the Security Onion monitoring destination IP is 10.10.10.10 on eth2, eth2 ideally being a dedicated interface.

On Security Onion:

- Enable Inverse repository for Security Onion:

```
sudo bash -c 'cat << EOL >/etc/apt/sources.list.d/securityonion-inverse.list
deb http://inverse.ca/downloads/PacketFence/securityonion trusty trusty
EOL'
```

```
gpg --keyserver keyserver.ubuntu.com --recv 19CDA6A9810273C4
gpg --export --armor 19CDA6A9810273C4 | sudo apt-key add -
```

- Install RCDCAP

```
sudo apt-get update
sudo apt-get install rcdcap
```

- Modify network file (/etc/network/inferfaces) so that eth2 has an IP and a proper MTU. Decapsulated traffic will be injected on mon1. Make sure that the configuration is similar to the following:

```
auto eth2
iface eth2 inet static
  address 10.10.10.10
  netmask 255.255.255.240
  up ip link set $IFACE arp on up
  up ip link set dev $IFACE mtu 1900
  post-up ethtool -G $IFACE rx 4096; for i in rx tx sg tso ufo gso gro lro; do
 ethtool -K $IFACE $i off; done
  post-up echo 1 > /proc/sys/net/ipv6/conf/$IFACE/disable_ipv6
```

```
auto mon1
iface mon1 inet manual
  pre-up rcdcap -i eth1 --erspan --tap-persist --tap-device $IFACE --expression
 "host 172.16.0.1" -d
  up ip link set $IFACE promisc on arp off up
  down ip link set $IFACE promisc off down
  post-up ethtool -G $IFACE rx ; for i in rx tx sg tso ufo gso gro lro; do
 ethtool -K $IFACE $i off; done
  post-up echo 1 > /proc/sys/net/ipv6/conf/$IFACE/disable_ipv6
```

- Rerun Security Onion wizard and make sure to skip network configuration step. Make sure that mon1 is selected for monitoring purposes, note that eth2 doesn't need to.

```
sudo sosetup
```

On the Switch:

```
monitor session 10 type erspan-source
description ERSPAN to 10.10.10.10
source interface GigabitEthernet0/10
destination
erspan-id 10
ip address 10.10.10.10
origin ip address 172.16.0.1
no shutdown   !  Default is shutdown
```

# Violations

In order to make PacketFence react to the Snort alerts, you need to explicitly tell the software to do so. Otherwise, the alerts will be discarded. This is quite simple to accomplish. In fact, you need to create a violation and add the Snort alert SID in the trigger section of a Violation.

PacketFence violations are configured in *Configuration→Compliance→Violations*

The example below will guide you to create a violation that will isolate device that have generated Peer-to-peer traffic and that are using Mac OSX or have a malware and are using Microsoft Windows

## Violation definition

First you need to configure the violation definition

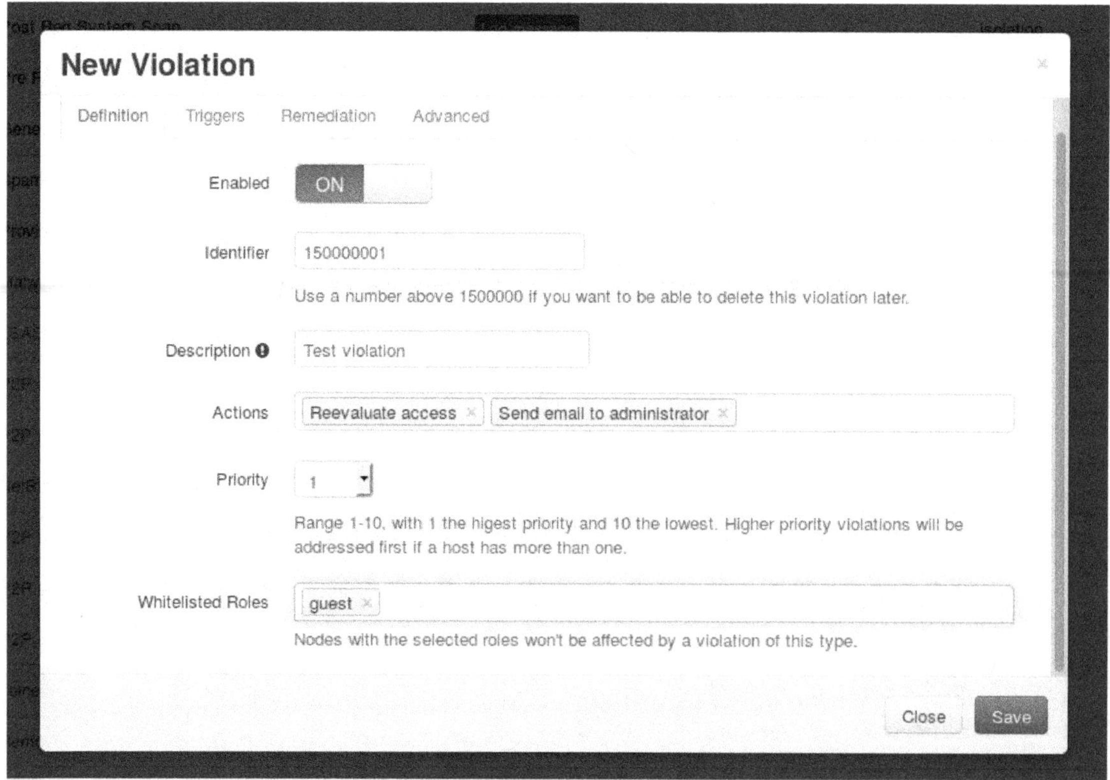


Where :

- `Enabled` is whether or not the violation is currently activated (should be `ON`).
- `Identifier` is the violation ID. Any integer except 1200000-120099 which is reserved for required administration violations.
- `Description` is the user friendly description of the violation.
- `Actions` is the list of actions to be executed when this violation is raised.

  - `Unregister node` will unregister the node.

  - `Send email to owner` will email the violation details to the owner of the device. Will only work if the person has it's email field populated.

  - `Send email to admin` will email the violation details to the address specified in `[alerting].emailaddr`, using `[alerting].smtpserver`. Multiple `emailaddr` can be separated by comma.

  - `Reevaluate access` will place the device in the destination VLAN configured in the violation. It opens a violation and leaves it open. If it is not there, the violation is opened and then automatically closed.

  - `Log message` will log the violation in the log file violation.log.

  - `External command` will execute a command on the operating system when this violation is raised.

  - `Close a violation` will close an existing violation for this device when this one is raised.

  - `Set role` will modify the role of the device.

  - `Enforce provisioning` will trigger a check of compliance on the provisioners defined for the device.
- `Priority` defines the order onto which violations should be handled should there be more than one for a device.
- `Whitelisted Roles` is the list of roles that are not affected by this violation.

## Triggers

Next, in the `Triggers` tab, you need to define the triggers that will raise the violation. In the case of this example it will be these two cases : * A device that has generated Peer-to-peer traffic and that is using MAC OSX. * A device that has been detected as being a rogue DHCP.

Click the `+` sign at the top right in order to create a new trigger, then in the dropdown select `Suricata`.

A menu will appear into which you can select `ET P2P` which will match all P2P alerts from Suricata.

Once you added this trigger, select `Device` from the dropdown and enter `38` which is the device identifier for Mac OSX.

Next hit the `<` button, then the `+` to add another trigger.

Select the type `Internal`, then in the menu that appears below it, select `Rogue DHCP detection` and click `Add`.

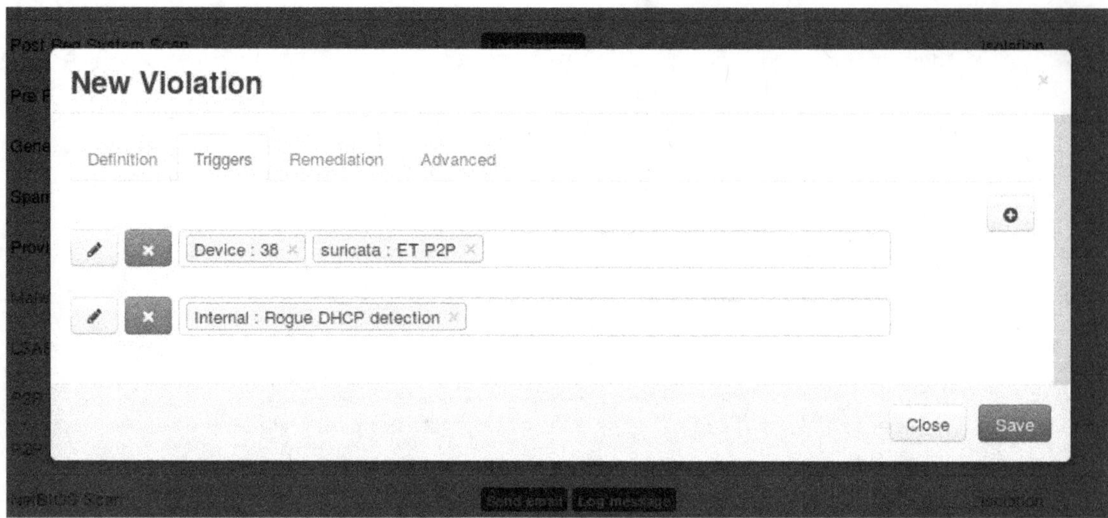


## Remediation

Next, in the **`Remediation`** tab, you can configure the behavior when a client gets isolated.

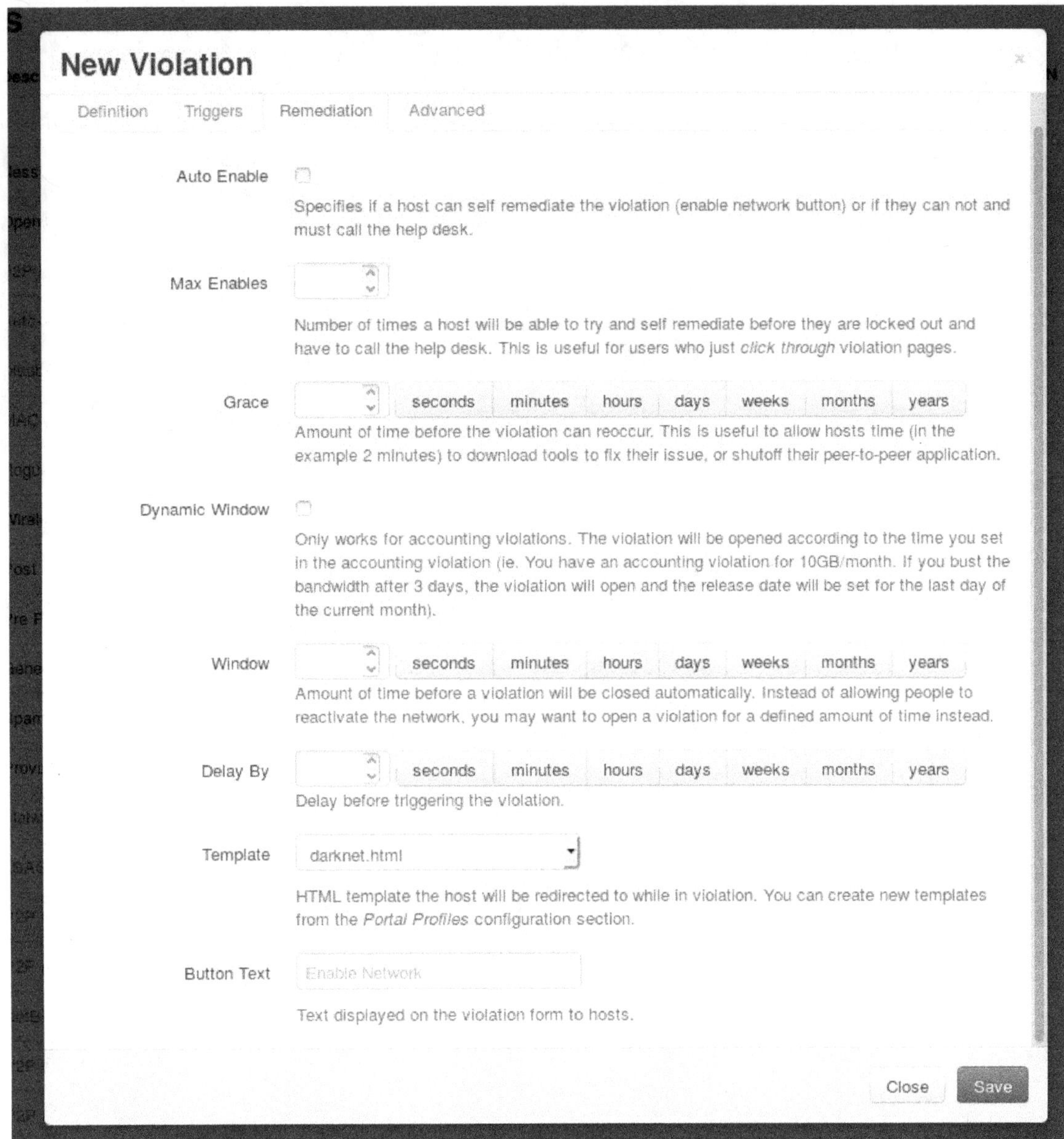


Where :

- `Auto Enable` is whether or not the user can release the violation himself after acknowledging the message on the captive portal.
- `Max Enables` is the amount of time a user can use the `Auto Enable` functionality. After this amount of times, he will not be able to release the violation and it will have to be manually release by an administrator using the PacketFence administration interface.
- `Grace` is Amount of time before the violation can reoccur. This is useful to allow hosts time (in the example 2 minutes) to download tools to fix their issue, or shutoff their peer-to-peer application.
- `Dynamic Window` will only works for accounting violations. The violation will be opened according to the time you set in the accounting violation (ie. You have an accounting violation for 10GB/ month. If you bust the bandwidth after 3 days, the violation will open and the release date will be set for the last day of the current month).
- `Window` is the amount of time before a violation will be closed automatically. Instead of allowing people to reactivate the network, you may want to open a violation for a defined amount of time instead.

- `Delay by` is the delay before triggering the violation.
- `Template` is the HTML template the host will be redirected to while in violation. You can create new templates from the Connection Profiles configuration section.
- `Button text` is the text of the button that is used when the user is releasing the violation directly from the captive portal.

### Advanced

In the **`Advanced`** tab you configure the destination VLAN of the device when it has the **`Reevaluate access`** action and its redirection URL when the user is released.

# Compliance Checks

PacketFence supports either Nessus, OpenVAS and WMI as a scanning engine for compliance checks. Since PacketFence v5.1 you are now able to create multiples scan engines configuration and assign them on specific captive portals. It mean per example that you are now able to active a scan for specific Operating System only on a specific SSID.

## Installation

### Nessus

Please visit http://www.nessus.org/download/ to download Nessus v5 and install the Nessus package for your operating system. You will also need to register for the HomeFeed (or the ProfessionalFeed) in order to get the plugins.

After you installed Nessus, follow the Nessus documentation for the configuration of the Nessus Server, and to create a user for PacketFence.

Note

You may run into some issue while using Nessus with the Net::Nessus::XMLRPC module (which is the default behavior in PacketFence). Please refer to the bug tracking system for more information.

### OpenVAS

Please visit http://www.openvas.org/install-packages.html#openvas4_centos_atomic to configure the correct repository to be able to install the latest OpenVAS scanning engine.

Once installed, please make sure to follow the instructions to correctly configure the scanning engine and create a scan configuration that will fit your needs. You'll also need to create a user for PacketFence to be able to communicate with the server.

It is important to get the correct scan config ID and NBE report format ID to populate the parameters in the PacketFence configuration file. The easiest way to get these IDs is by downloading both of the scan configuration and report format from the OpenVAS web gui and retrieve the IDs in the filenames.

For example `report-format-f5c2a364-47d2-4700-b21d-0a7693daddab.xml` gives report format ID `f5c2a364-47d2-4700-b21d-0a7693daddab`.

### WMI

You just have to enable wmi on each windows devices with a GPO from Active Directory.

## Configuration

In order for the compliance checks to correctly work with PacketFence (communication and generate violations inside PacketFence), you need to configure these sections:

### Scanner Definition

First go in Configuration and Scanner Definition: *Configuration→Compliance→Scans Engines*

Then add a scan:

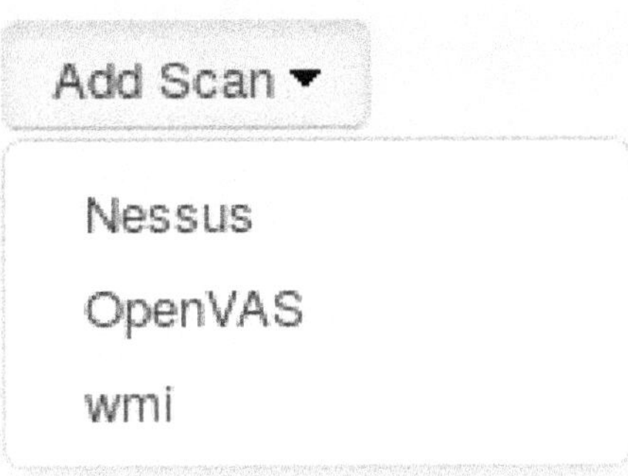


There are common parameters for each scan engines:

```
Name: the name of your scan engine
Roles: Only devices with these role(s) will be affected (Optional)
OS: Only devices with this Operating System will be affected (Optional)
Duration: Approximate duration of scan (Progress bar on the captive portal)
Scan before registration: Trigger the scan when the device appear on the
 registration vlan
Scan after registration: Trigger the scan just after registration on the captive
 portal
Scan after registration: Trigger the scan on the production network
 (pfdhcplistener must receive production dhcp traffic)
802.1X: Even if the auto-registration has been enabled, the scan will be trigger
 on a EAP connection
802.1X types: comma delimited EAP type that will trigger the scan if 802.1X above
 has been enabled
```

Specific to Nessus:

```
Hostname or IP Address: Hostname or IP Address where Nessus is running
Username: Username to connect to Nessus scan
Password: Password to connect to Nessus scan
Port of the service: port to connect (default 8834)
Nessus client policy: the name of the policy to use for the scan (Must be define
 on the Nessus server)
```

Specific to OpenVAS:

```
Hostname or IP Address: Hostname or IP Address where OpenVAS is running
Username: Username to connect to OpenVAS scan
Password: Password to connect to OpenVAS scan
Port of the service: port to connect (default 9390)
OpenVAS config ID: the ID of scanning configuration on the OpenVAS server
```

Specific to WMI:

```
Username: A username from Active Directory that is allowed to connect to wmi
Domain: Domain of the Active Directory
Password: Password of the account
WMI Rules: Ordered list of WMI rules you defined in Configuration -> Compliance -
> Scans -> WMI Rules
```

## WMI Rules Definition

If you have configured a WMI scan engine then you need to define WMI Rules. WMI is a sort of database on each windows devices, to retrieve information on the device you need to know the sql request. In order to help you to find and make a rule you can use a third party tool like WMI Explorer.

Go in configuration → WMI Rules Definition:

There are already 3 rules defined:

```
Software_Installed
logged_user
Process_Running
```

Let's take the Software_Installed rule:

```
request: select * from Win32_Product
```

```
Rules Actions:
```

```
[Google]
attribute = Caption
operator = match
value =Google
```

```
[1:Google]
action=trigger_violation
action_param = mac = $mac, tid = 888888, type = INTERNAL
```

This rule will do the following:

```
retrieve all the installed software on the device and test if the attribute
 Caption contain Google.
if it matched then we will trigger a violation (with the trigger
 internal::888888) for the mac address of the device.
```

The second one, logged_user:

```
request: select UserName from Win32_ComputerSystem
```

```
Rules Actions:
```

```
[UserName]
attribute = UserName
operator = match
value = (.*)
```

```
[1:UserName]
action = dynamic_register_node
action_param = mac = $mac, username = $result->{'UserName'}
```

This rule will do the following:

```
retrieve the current logged user on the device and register the device based on
 the user account.
```

The last one, Process_Running:

```
request: select Name from Win32_Process
```

```
Rules Actions:
```

```
[explorer]
attribute = Name
operator = match
value = explorer.exe
```

```
[1:explorer]
action = allow
```

This rule will do the following:

```
retrieve all the running process on the device and if one match explorer.exe then
 we bypass the scan.
```

- Rules syntax

```
the syntax of the rules are simple to understand:
```

```
the request is the sql request you will launch on the remote device, you must
 know what the request will return
to write the test.
```

```
Inside the Rules Actions we define 2 sorts of blocs:
The test bloc (ie [explorer]) and the action bloc (ie [1:explorer])
```

```
The test bloc is a simple test based on the result of the request:
- attribute is the attribute you want to test
- operator can be:
  is
  is_not
  match
  match_not
- value is the value you want to compare
```

```
Feel free to define multiples test blocs
```

```
The action bloc is where you will define your logic, per example let's take
 this one [1:google&explorer], this mean that if the google test is
true and explorer is true then we execute the action.
The logic can be more complex and can be something like that [1:!google|
(explorer&memory)] that mean if not google or (explorer and memory)
```

### WMI tab:

From PacketFence 6.4 it is possible to have the result of a WMI scan in the node section. To have this, go into the rule configuration and check the box *On Node tab*. Now configure your WMI scanner as you would usually do and you will be able to have the results in the tab *WMI Rules* under Node.

### Violations definition

You need to create a new violation section and have to specify:

Using Nessus:

```
trigger=Nessus::<violationId>
```

Using OpenVAS:

```
trigger=OpenVAS::<violationId>
```

Where `violationId` is either the ID of the Nessus plugin or the OID of the OpenVAS plugin to check for. Once you have finished the configuration, you need to reload the violation related database contents using:

```
$ pfcmd reload violations
```

Note

Violations will trigger if the plugin is higher than a low severity vulnerability.

### Assign Scan definition to connection profiles

The last step is to assign one or more scanner you configured to one or more connection profiles. Go in Configuration → Policies and Access Control → Connection Profiles → Edit a Profile → Add Scan

## Hosting Nessus / OpenVAS remotely

Because of the CPU intensive nature of an automated vulnerability assessment, we recommend that it is hosted on a separate server for large environments. To do so, a couple of things are required:

- PacketFence needs to be able to communicate to the server on the port specified by the vulnerability engine used
- The scanning server need to be able to access the targets. In other words, registration VLAN access is required if scan on registration is enabled.

If you are using the OpenVAS scanning engine:

- The scanning server need to be able to reach PacketFence's Admin interface (on port 1443 by default) by its DNS entry. Otherwise PacketFence won't be notified of completed scans.
- You must have a valid SSL certificate on your PacketFence server

If you are using the Nessus scanning engine:

- You just have to change the host value by the Nessus server IP.

# RADIUS Accounting

RADIUS Accounting is usually used by ISPs to bill clients. In PacketFence, we are able to use this information to determine if the node is still connected, how much time it has been connected, and how much bandwidth the user consumed.

## Violations

Using PacketFence, it is possible to add violations to limit bandwidth abuse. The format of the trigger is very simple:

```
Accounting::[DIRECTION][LIMIT][INTERVAL(optional)]
```

Let's explain each chunk properly:

- `DIRECTION`: You can either set a limit to inbound(IN), outbound(OUT), or total(TOT) bandwidth
- `LIMIT`: You can set a number of bytes(B), kilobytes(KB), megabytes(MB), gigabytes(GB), or petabytes(PB)
- `INTERVAL`: This is actually the time window we will look for potential abuse. You can set a number of days(D), weeks(W), months(M), or years(Y).

### Example triggers

- Look for Incoming (Download) traffic with a 50GB/month

  ```
  Accounting::IN50GB1M
  ```

- Look for Outgoing (Upload) traffic with a 500MB/day

  ```
  Accounting::OUT500MB1D
  ```

- Look for Total (Download + Upload) traffic with a 200GB limit in the last week

  ```
  Accounting::TOT200GB1W
  ```

### Grace period

When using such violation feature, setting the grace period is really important. You don't want to put it too low (ie. A user re-enable his network, and get caught after 1 bytes is transmitted!) or too high. We recommend that you set the grace period to one interval window.

# Oinkmaster

Oinkmaster is a perl script that enables the possibility to update the different snort rules very easily. It is simple to use, and install. This section will show you how to implement Oinkmaster to work with PacketFence and Snort.

Please visit http://oinkmaster.sourceforge.net/download.shtml to download oinkmaster. A sample oinkmaster configuration file is provided at `/usr/local/pf/addons/snort/oinkmaster.conf`.

## Configuration

Here are the steps to make Oinkmaster work. We will assume that you already downloaded the newest oinkmaster archive:

1. Untar the freshly downloaded Oinkmaster
2. Copy the required perl scripts into `/usr/local/pf/oinkmaster`. You need to copy over `contrib` and `oinkmaster.pl`
3. Copy the `oinkmaster.conf` provided by PacketFence (see the section above) in `/usr/local/pf/conf`
4. Modify the configuration to suit your own needs. Currently, the configuration file is set to fetch the bleeding rules.

## Rules update

In order to get periodic updates for PacketFence Snort rules, we simply need to create a `crontab` entry with the right information. The example below shows a `crontab` entry to fetch the updates daily at 23:00 PM:

```
0 23 * * * (cd /usr/local/pf; perl oinkmaster/oinkmaster.pl -C conf/
oinkmaster.conf -o conf/snort/)
```

# Guests Management

PacketFence supports the ability to manage guests by establishing expire dates and assign different roles which will permit different accesses to the network resources.

Guests can self-register themselves using an activation code sent to their mobile phone or they can use their email address and receive and activation link to activate their network access.

PacketFence has the option to have guests sponsored their access by local staff. Once a guest requests a sponsored access an email is sent to the sponsor and the sponsor must click on a link and authenticate in order to enable his access.

Moreover, PacketFence also has the option for guests to request their access in advance. Confirmation by email and by a sponsor are the two pre-registration techniques supported at this point.

The admin GUI allow PacketFence administrators or guests managers to create single accounts, multiple accounts using a prefix (ie.: guest1, guest2, guest3...) or import data from a CSV to create accounts. Access duration and expected arrival date are also customizable.

# Usage

## Guest self-registration

Self-registration is enabled by default. It is part of the connection profile and can be accessed on the registration page by clicking the **Sign up** link.

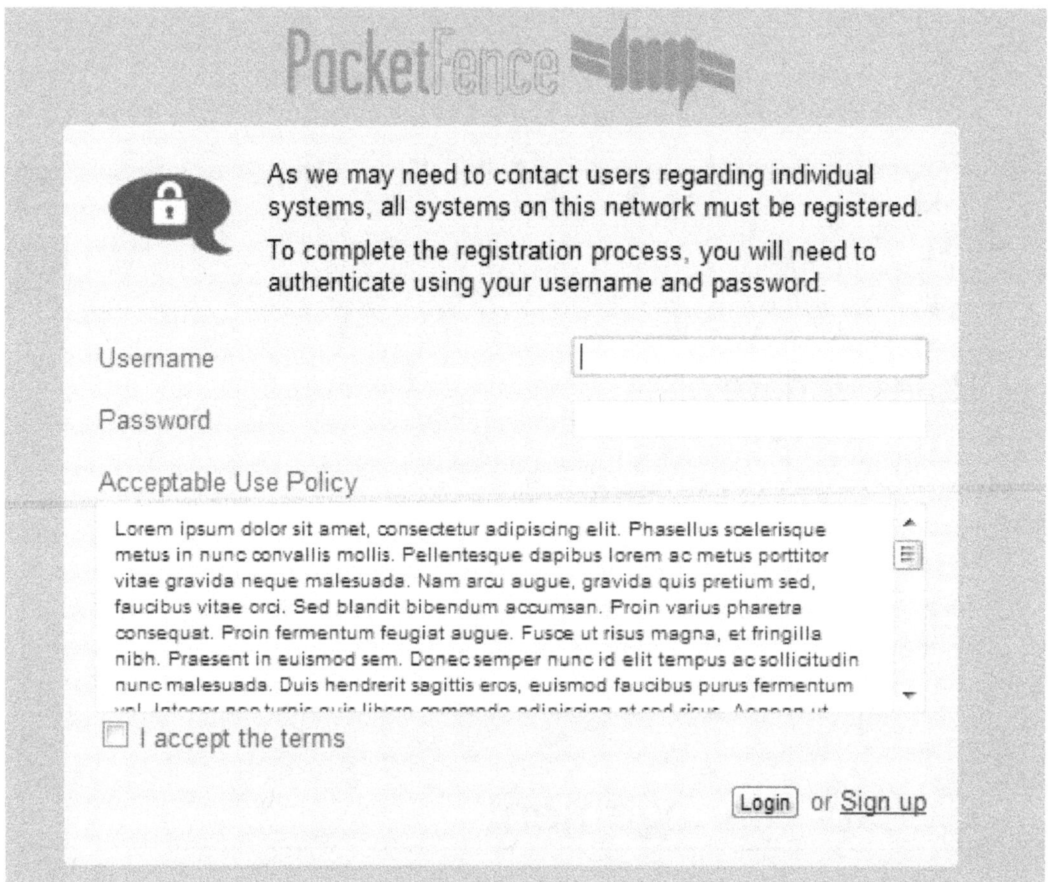


## Managed guests

Part of the web administration interface, the guests management interface is enabled by default. It is accessible through the **Users → Create** menu.

## Guest pre-registration

Pre-registration is disabled by default. Once enabled, PacketFence's firewall and Apache ACLs allow access to the **/signup** page on the portal even from a remote location. All that should be required from the administrators is to open up their perimeter firewall to allow access to PacketFence's management interface IP on port 443 and make sure a domain name to reach said IP is configured (and that the SSL cert matches it). Then you can promote the pre-registration link from your extranet web site: https://<hostname>/signup.

### Caution

Pre-registration increases the attack surface of the PacketFence system since a subset of it's functionality is exposed on the Internet. Make sure you understand the risks, apply the critical operating system updates and apply PacketFence's security fixes.

### Note

A *portal* interface type is required to use this feature. A *portal* interface type can be added to any network interface using the web admin GUI.

# Configuration

## Access Duration

Default values are located in `/usr/local/pf/conf/pf.conf.defaults` and documentation for every settings is available in `/usr/local/pf/conf/documentations.conf`.

```
[guests_admin_registration]
access_duration_choices=1h,3h,12h,1D,2D,3D,5D
default_access_duration=12h
```

The format of the duration is as follow:

```
<DURATION><DATETIME_UNIT>[<PERIOD_BASE><OPERATOR><DURATION><DATE_UNIT>]
```

Let's explain the meaning of each parameter:

- `DURATION`: a number corresponding to the period duration.
- `DATETIME_UNIT`: a character corresponding to the units of the date or time duration; either s (seconds), m (minutes), h (hours), D (days), W (weeks), M (months), or Y (years).
- `PERIOD_BASE`: either F (fixed) or R (relative). A relative period is computed from the beginning of the period unit. Weeks start on Monday.
- `OPERATOR`: either + or -. The duration following the operator is added or subtracted from the base duration.
- `DATE_UNIT`: a character corresponding to the units of the extended duration. Limited to date units (D (days), W (weeks), M (months), or Y (years)).

These parameters should be configured from the **Configuration → Advanced Access Configuration → Access Duration** section of the Web admin interface.

From the Users page of the PacketFence Web admin interface, it is possible to set the access duration of users, change their password and more.

## Guest pre-registration

To minimally configure guest pre-registration, you must make sure that the following statement is set under `[guests_self_registration]` in `/usr/local/pf/conf/pf.conf`:

```
[guests_self_registration]
preregistration=enabled
```

This parameter should be configured from the **Configuration → Policies and Access Control → Connection Profiles → Profile Name** section.

Finally, it is advised that you read the whole guest self-registration section since pre-registration is simply a twist of the self-registration process.

### Caution

A valid MTA configured in PacketFence is needed to correctly relay emails related to the guest module. If *localhost* is used as smtpserver, make sure that a MTA is installed and configured on the server.

# Active Directory Integration

## Deleted Account

Create the script `unreg_node_deleted_account.ps1` on the Windows Server with the following content. Make sure to change `@IP_PACKETFENCE` to the IP address of your PacketFence server. You'll also need to change the username and password as they must match the credentials defined in the Web admin interface under **Configuration → Advanced Access Configuration → Web Services**.

```
###########################################################################################
#Powershell script to unregister deleted Active Directory account based on the
 UserName.#
###########################################################################################

Get-EventLog -LogName Security -InstanceId 4726 |
   Select ReplacementStrings,"Account name"|
   % {
    $url = "https://@IP_PACKETFENCE:9090/"
    $username = "admin" # Username for the webservices
    $password = "admin" # Password for the webservices
    [System.Net.ServicePointManager]::ServerCertificateValidationCallback =
 {$true}
    $command = '{"jsonrpc": "2.0", "method": "unreg_node_for_pid", "params":
 ["pid", "'+$_.ReplacementStrings[0]+'"]}'

    $bytes = [System.Text.Encoding]::ASCII.GetBytes($command)
    $web = [System.Net.WebRequest]::Create($url)
    $web.Method = "POST"
    $web.ContentLength = $bytes.Length
    $web.ContentType = "application/json-rpc"
    $web.Credentials = new-object System.Net.NetworkCredential($username,
 $password)
    $stream = $web.GetRequestStream()
    $stream.Write($bytes,0,$bytes.Length)
    $stream.close()

    $reader = New-Object System.IO.Streamreader -ArgumentList
 $web.GetResponse().GetResponseStream()
    $reader.ReadToEnd()
    $reader.Close()
   }
```

## Create the scheduled task based on an event ID

Start → Run → Taskschd.msc

Task Scheduler → Task Scheduler Library → Event Viewer Task → Create Task

General

```
Name: PacketFence-Unreg_node-for-deleted-account
Check: Run whether user is logged on or not
Check: Run with highest privileges
```

Triggers → New

```
Begin on the task: On an event
Log: Security
Source: Microsoft Windows security auditing.
Event ID: 4726
```

Actions → New

```
Action: Start a program
Program/script: powershell.exe
Add arguments (optional): C:\scripts\unreg_node_deleted_account.ps1
```

Settings:

```
At the bottom, select in the list "Run a new instance in parallel" in order to
 unregister multiple nodes at the same time.
```

Validate with Ok and give the account who will run this task. (Usually *DOMAIN\Administrator*)

## Disabled Account

Create the script `unreg_node_disabled_account.ps1` on the Windows Server with the following content. Make sure to change `@IP_PACKETFENCE` to the IP address of your PacketFence server. You'll also need to change the username and password as they must match the credentials defined in the Web admin interface under **Configuration → Advanced Access Configuration → Web Services**.

```
#########################################################################################
#Powershell script to unregister disabled Active Directory account based on the
 UserName.#
#########################################################################################

Get-EventLog -LogName Security -InstanceId 4725 |
   Select ReplacementStrings,"Account name"|
   % {
    $url = "https://@IP_PACKETFENCE:9090/"
    $username = "admin" # Username for the webservices
    $password = "admin" # Password for the webservices
    [System.Net.ServicePointManager]::ServerCertificateValidationCallback =
 {$true}
    $command = '{"jsonrpc": "2.0", "method": "unreg_node_for_pid", "params":
 ["pid", "'+$_.ReplacementStrings[0]+'"]}'

    $bytes = [System.Text.Encoding]::ASCII.GetBytes($command)
    $web = [System.Net.WebRequest]::Create($url)
    $web.Method = "POST"
    $web.ContentLength = $bytes.Length
    $web.ContentType = "application/json-rpc"
    $web.Credentials = new-object System.Net.NetworkCredential($username,
 $password)
    $stream = $web.GetRequestStream()
    $stream.Write($bytes,0,$bytes.Length)
    $stream.close()

    $reader = New-Object System.IO.Streamreader -ArgumentList
 $web.GetResponse().GetResponseStream()
    $reader.ReadToEnd()
    $reader.Close()

   }
```

## Create the scheduled task based on an event ID

**Start → Run → Taskschd.msc**

**Task Scheduler → Task Scheduler Library → Event Viewer Task → Create Task**

General

```
Name: PacketFence-Unreg_node-for-disabled-account
Check: Run whether user is logged on or not
Check: Run with highest privileges
```

Triggers → New

```
Begin on the task: On an event
Log: Security
Source: Microsoft Windows security auditing.
Event ID: 4725
```

Actions → New

```
Action: Start a program
Program/script: powershell.exe
Add arguments (optional): C:\scripts\unreg_node_disabled_account.ps1
```

Settings:

```
At the bottom, select in the list "Run a new instance in parallel"
```

Validate with Ok and give the account who will run this task. (Usually *DOMAIN\Administrator*)

# Locked Account

Create the script `unreg_node_locked_account.ps1` on the Windows Server with the following content. Make sure to change `@IP_PACKETFENCE` to the IP address of your PacketFence server. You'll also need to change the username and password as they must match the credentials defined in the Web admin interface under **Configuration → Advanced Access Configuration → Web Services**.

```
##########################################################################################
#Powershell script to unregister locked Active Directory account based on the
 UserName.#
##########################################################################################

Get-EventLog -LogName Security -InstanceId 4740 |
   Select ReplacementStrings,"Account name"|
   % {
    $url = "https://@IP_PACKETFENCE:9090/"
    $username = "admin" # Username for the webservices
    $password = "admin" # Password for the webservices
    [System.Net.ServicePointManager]::ServerCertificateValidationCallback =
 {$true}
    $command = '{"jsonrpc": "2.0", "method": "unreg_node_for_pid", "params":
 ["pid", "'+$_.ReplacementStrings[0]+'"]}'

    $bytes = [System.Text.Encoding]::ASCII.GetBytes($command)
    $web = [System.Net.WebRequest]::Create($url)
    $web.Method = "POST"
    $web.ContentLength = $bytes.Length
    $web.ContentType = "application/json-rpc"
    $web.Credentials = new-object System.Net.NetworkCredential($username,
 $password)
    $stream = $web.GetRequestStream()
    $stream.Write($bytes,0,$bytes.Length)
    $stream.close()

    $reader = New-Object System.IO.Streamreader -ArgumentList
 $web.GetResponse().GetResponseStream()
    $reader.ReadToEnd()
    $reader.Close()

   }
```

## Create the scheduled task based on an event ID

Start → Run → Taskschd.msc

Task Scheduler → Task Scheduler Library → Event Viewer Task → Create Task

General

```
Name: PacketFence-Unreg_node-for-locked-account
Check: Run whether user is logged on or not
Check: Run with highest privileges
```

Triggers → New

```
Begin on the task: On an event
Log: Security
Source: Microsoft Windows security auditing.
Event ID: 4740
```

Actions → New

```
Action: Start a program
Program/script: powershell.exe
Add arguments (optional): C:\scripts\unreg_node_locked_account.ps1
```

Settings:

```
At the bottom, select in the list "Run a new instance in parallel"
```

Validate with Ok and give the account who will run this task. (Usually *DOMAIN\Administrator*)

# DHCP remote sensor

The DHCP remote sensor consists of a lightweight binary that is installed on your production DHCP server in order to replicate the DHCP traffic 1 to 1 to the PacketFence server. This solution is more reliable than the DHCP relaying since PacketFence receives a copy of all your DHCP traffic and not only the broadcasted DHCP traffic. Supported DHCP servers are Microsoft DHCP server and CentOS 6 and 7.

These sensors work by capturing the packets at the lowest level possible on your DHCP server and forward them to the PacketFence management interface

## Microsoft DHCP sensor

DHCP-Forwarder is an optimized version of precedent udp-reflector, which installs easily and only copy DHCPREQUESTS and DHCPACK packets to the destination.

Download the installer here.

It will install WinPCAP, nssm, launch a configurator to ask for interface, IP and port, save the configuration, install and launch DHCP-Forwarder service.

When you will be asked for a host IP and port, specify PacketFence management IP and 767 as the UDP port.

The project page can be found here.

## Linux based sensor

First download the RPM on your DHCP server.

### CentOS 6 and 7 servers

For CentOS 6:

```
# for x86_64
# wget http://inverse.ca/downloads/PacketFence/CentOS6/extra/x86_64/RPMS/udp-
reflector-1.0-6.1.x86_64.rpm
```

For CentOS 7:

```
# for x86_64
# wget http://inverse.ca/downloads/PacketFence/CentOS7/extra/x86_64/RPMS/udp-
reflector-1.0-6.1.x86_64.rpm
```

Now install the sensor:

```
# rpm -i udp-reflector-*.rpm
```

## Compiling the sensor from source on a Linux system

First make sure you have the following packages installed:

- libpcap
- libpcap-devel
- gcc-c++

Get the source code of the sensor:

```
# mkdir -p ~/udp-reflector && cd ~/udp-reflector
# wget http://inverse.ca/downloads/PacketFence/udp-reflector/udp_reflector.cpp
# g++ udp_reflector.cpp -o /usr/local/bin/udp_reflector -lpcap
```

## Configuring the sensor

Place the following line in `/etc/rc.local`

- where `pcap0` is the pcap interface where your DHCP server listens on. (List them using `udp_reflector -l`)
- where `192.168.1.5` is the management IP of your PacketFence server

```
/usr/local/bin/udp_reflector -s pcap0:67 -d 192.168.1.5:767 -b 25000 &
```

Start the sensor:

```
# /usr/local/bin/udp_reflector -s pcap0:67 -d 192.168.1.5:767 -b 25000 &
```

The DHCP traffic should now be reflected on your PacketFence server.

# Switch login access

PacketFence is able to act as an authentication and authorization service on the port 1815 for granting command-line interface (CLI) access to switches. PacketFence currently supports Cisco switches and these must be configured using the following guide: http://www.cisco.com/c/en/us/support/docs/security-vpn/remote-authentication-dial-user-service-radius/116291-configure-freeradius-00.html From the PacketFence's web admin interface, you must configure an Admin Access role (Configuration→Network Configuration→Admin access) that contains the action *Switches CLI - Read* or *Switches CLI - Write* and assign this role to an internal user or in an Administration rule in an internal source.

## DHCP Option 82

PacketFence is able to locate a device on the network even if the switch port is not managed by PacketFence. To use this feature you need to add all the switches in PacketFence and enable SNMP read (switch and PacketFence side) and enable DHCP option 82 in Configuration → Network Configuration → Networks → Network. Once enabled, restart the pfdhcplistener and pfmon services. pfmon will query via SNMP all the switches to create a map (MAC <→ switch) pfdhcplistener will parse the DHCP Option 82 and will use the map to resolve the MAC to the switch and will update the locationlog of the device.

## Trigger a violation when discovering a node

PacketFence is able to trigger a violation when a node is discovered on your network. It will send the trigger internal::node_discovered which is already part of violation 1300004. You can enable this violation with the default values and it will send a short report for every new device discovered by PacketFence. You can also execute any typical violation actions on during this process.

# Best Practices

## RHEL7 systemd early swapoff bug mitigation

A known bug is still present in systemd-219-30.el7_3.7.x86_64 shipped with CentOS. (Debian fixed it in 228-3).

The bug arises because not all swap aliases are registered, which results in an incorrect dependence tree which results in swapoff being called way too early at shutdown.

### Workaround

- Obtain the list of swap items that should be considered by systemd for it to enforce a correct ordering:

```
#grep swap /var/log/dmesg |grep "dead -> active"
```

In our example, that gave the following output:

``` [ 1.995413] systemd[1]: dev-dm\x2d1.swap changed dead → active [ 1.995495] systemd[1]: dev-cl-swap.swap changed dead → active [ 1.995550] systemd[1]: dev-disk-by\x2did-dm\x2dname\x2dcl\x2dswap.swap changed dead → active [ 1.995616] systemd[1]: dev-disk-by\x2did-dm\x2duuid\x2dLVM \x2dXOAK7DHxMdmQCrNdwWE3Pt836Q9pHYSGyrO9ycCGelYavzbamVWNKMaVUMLf1NWZ.swap changed dead → active [ 1.995678] systemd[1]: dev-disk-by\x2duuid-6509e6e1\x2daf2d \x2d4d23\x2d9ebd\x2da9aa8801e658.swap changed dead → active ```

- Create /etc/systemd/system/swap.target and fill it with all swap aliases obtained from the previous command:

```

Description=Swap Documentation=man:systemd.special(7) After=dev-disk-by \x2duuid-6509e6e1\x2daf2d\x2d4d23\x2d9ebd\x2da9aa8801e658.swap dev-dm1.swap dev-disk-by\x2did-dm\x2duuid\x2dLVM \x2dXOAK7DHxMdmQCrNdwWE3Pt836Q9pHYSGyrO9ycCGelYavzbamVWNKMaVUMLf1NWZ.swap dev-disk-by\x2did-dm\x2dname\x2dcl\x2dswap.swap dev-cl-swap.swap dev-dm\x2d1.swap ```

# Operating System Best Practices

## IPTables

IPTables is now entirely managed by PacketFence. However, if you need to perform some custom rules, you can modify **conf/iptables.conf** to your own needs. However, the default template should work for most users.

## Log Rotations

PacketFence can generate a lot of log entries in huge production environments. This is why we recommend to use **logrotate** to periodically rotate your logs. A working logrotate script is provided with the PacketFence package. This script is located under the **/usr/local/pf/packetfence.logrotate** file, and it's configured to do a daily log rotation and keeping old logs with compression. It has been added during PacketFence initial installation.

 

# Performance optimization

## NTLM authentication caching

Note

This section assumes that you already have an Active Directory domain configuration both in *Configuration→Policies and Access Control→Domains→Active Directory Domains* and *Configuration→Policies and Access Control→Sources*. If you don't, you need to first configure those. Refer to the appropriate sections of this guide for details on how to configure those two components.

Caution

The cache requires minimally Windows Server 2008. Older versions will not work.

When using NTLM authentication against an Active Directory for 802.1X EAP-PEAP connections, this can become a bottleneck when handling dozens of authentications per seconds.

To overcome this limitation, it is possible to use a Redis driven cache inside PacketFence to reduce the amount of authentications requiring an external NTLM authentication call. Should a user be in the cache, PacketFence will attempt to compare the 802.1X credentials with those. In the even that the validation fails, a call to ntlm_auth is made. In the event of a cache miss, an ntlm_auth call is made as well. This ensures that even if a user changes his password, his new password is immediately valid for 802.1X EAP-PEAP connections even if the cache contains the outdated entry.

Note

The NTLM cache doesn't cache clear text passwords, it caches the NT hash of the user password.

### Additional packages

In order to use this cache, you will need to install additional packages available from the packetfence-extra repository. These packages will allow PacketFence to query your Active Directory for the NT hash of the users.

CentOS: ``` yum install python2-impacket --enablerepo=packetfence-extra ```

Debian: ``` apt-get install python-impacket ```

## PacketFence configuration

First of all, you will need to enable the NTLM caching globally by enabling *NTLM Redis cache* in *Configuration→System Configuration→Main Configuration→Advanced*. You then need to restart radiusd.

Once that is done, you need to configure PacketFence to start caching the credentials. In order to do so, go in *Configuration→Policies and Access Control→Domains→Active Directory Domains* and select the domain you want to cache the credentials for.

Next, go in the *NTLM cache* tab and:

- Enable *NTLM cache*
- Select the Active Directory authentication source that is tied to this domain.
- Adjust the *LDAP filter* if necessary. Note that this is only used for the batch job.
- Adjust the *Expiration*
- Enable *NTLM cache background job* and/or *NTLM cache on connection*. In the case of this example, both will be enabled.

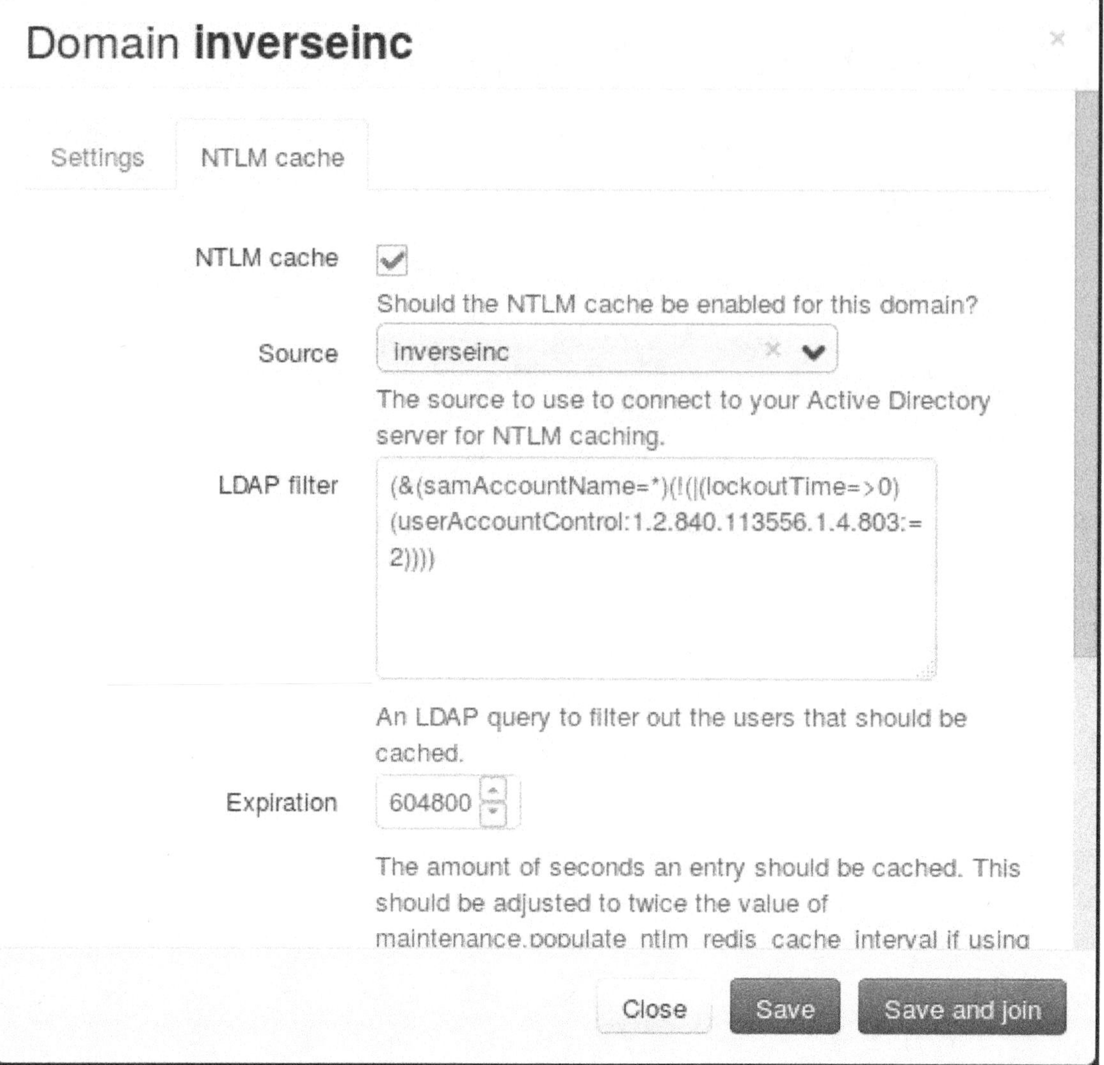
Domain inverseinc
Settings
NTLM cache
NTLM cache
Should the NTLM cache be enabled for this domain?
Source
inverseinc
The source to use to connect to your Active Directory server for NTLM caching.
LDAP filter
(&(samAccountName=*)(!(|(lockoutTime=>0)(userAccountControl:1.2.840.113556.1.4.803:=2))))
An LDAP query to filter out the users that should be cached.
Expiration
604800
The amount of seconds an entry should be cached. This should be adjusted to twice the value of
Close
Save
Save and join

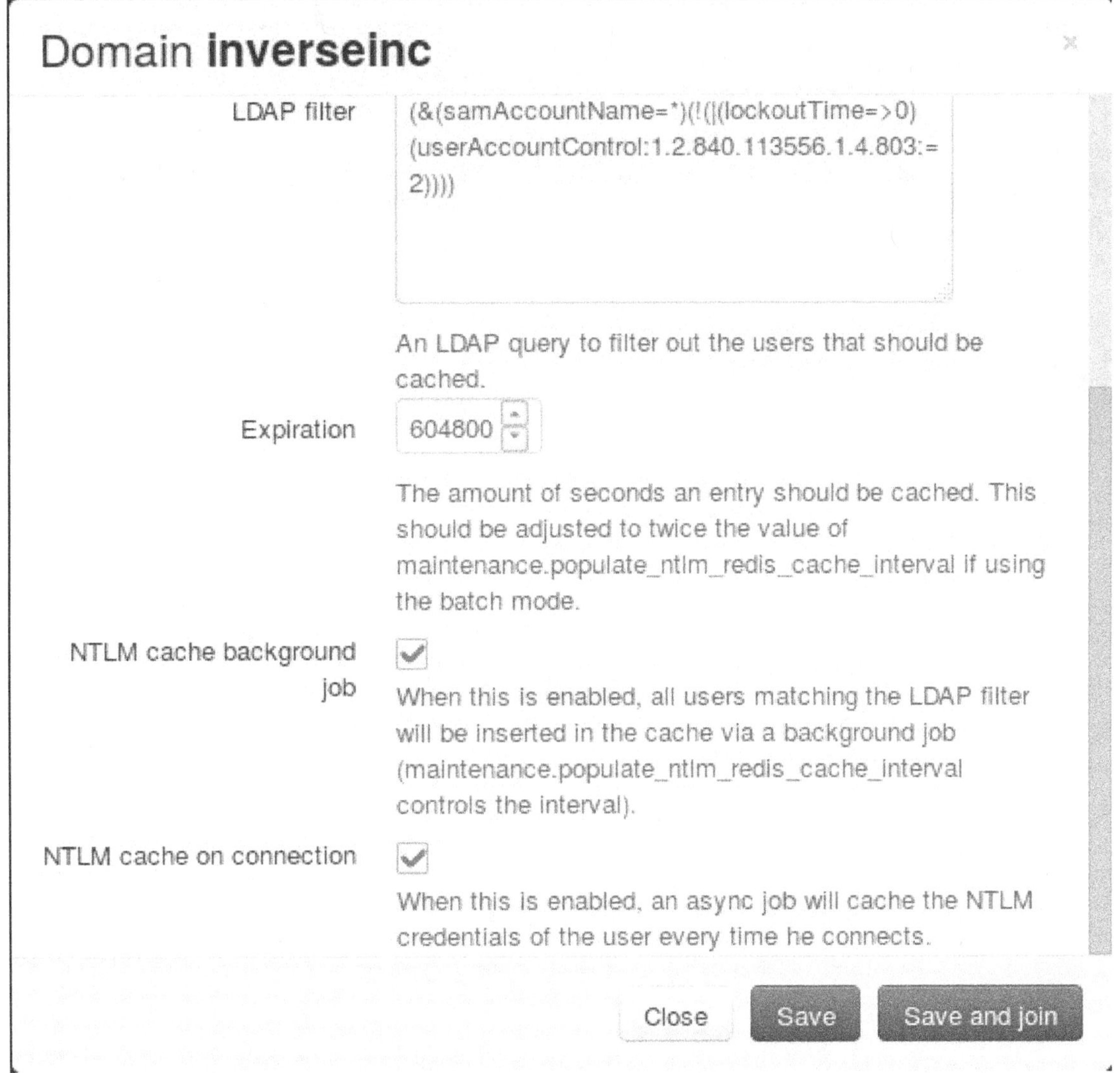


Once done, click *Save* to commit your changes.

After that, you will need to enable the 'redis_ntlm_cache` service which is used by PacketFence to store the cached credentials. In order to do so, go in Configuration→Main Configuration→Services' and enable *redis_ntlm_cache* and save the changes.

Next, start the service via pfcmd:

```
/usr/local/pf/bin/pfcmd service redis_ntlm_cache start
```

If you chose to enable *NTLM cache background job* in one of your domains, you will need to enable the pfmon job that will periodically cache the credentials. This can be configured in *Configuration→System Configuration→Main Configuration→Maintenance→populate_ntlm_redis_cache*. It is advised to set the interval of this task to half the expiration of the credentials you have set in the domain configuration. This will ensure you have an optimal cache hit. Once done, restart the `pfmon` service.

## Active Directory configuration

In order for PacketFence to be able to fetch the NTLM credentials from your Active Directory, it will need a user who has replication rights. The user to which you have to grant the rights, is the one that is configured in the authentication source that you associated in the *NTLM cache* section of your domain.

Please refer to the following Microsoft KB entry to configure the replication rights: https://support.microsoft.com/en-us/kb/303972

# SNMP Traps Limit

PacketFence mainly rely on SNMP traps to communicate with equipment. Due to the fact that traps coming in from approved (configured) devices are all processed by the daemon, it is possible for someone who want to generate a certain load on the PacketFence server to force the generation of non-legitimate SNMP traps or a switch can randomly generate a high quantity of traps sent to PacketFence for an unknown reason.

Because of that, it is possible to limit the number of SNMP traps coming in from a single switch port and take action if that limit is reached. For example, if over 100 traps are received by PacketFence from the same switch port in a minute, the switch port will be shut and a notification email will be sent.

Here's the default config for the SNMP traps limit feature. As you can see, by default, PacketFence will log the abnormal activity after 100 traps from the same switch port in a minute. These configurations are in the `conf/pf.conf` file:

```
[snmp_traps]
trap_limit = enabled
trap_limit_threshold = 100
trap_limit_action =
```

Alternatively, you can configure these parameters from the PacketFence Web administrative GUI, in the **Configuration → Network Configuration → SNMP** section.

# MySQL optimizations

## Tuning MySQL

If you're PacketFence system is acting very slow, this could be due to your MySQL configuration. You should do the following to tune performance:

Check the system load

```
# uptime
11:36:37 up 235 days,  1:21,  1 user, load average: 1.25, 1.05, 0.79
```

Check iostat and CPU

```
# iostat 5
avg-cpu:  %user   %nice    %sys %iowait   %idle
           0.60    0.00    3.20   20.20   76.00
Device:            tps   Blk_read/s   Blk_wrtn/s   Blk_read   Blk_wrtn
cciss/c0d0       32.40         0.00      1560.00          0       7800
avg-cpu:  %user   %nice    %sys %iowait   %idle
           0.60    0.00    2.20    9.20   88.00
Device:            tps   Blk_read/s   Blk_wrtn/s   Blk_read   Blk_wrtn
cciss/c0d0        7.80         0.00        73.60          0        368
avg-cpu:  %user   %nice    %sys %iowait   %idle
           0.60    0.00    1.80   23.80   73.80
Device:            tps   Blk_read/s   Blk_wrtn/s   Blk_read   Blk_wrtn
cciss/c0d0       31.40         0.00      1427.20          0       7136
avg-cpu:  %user   %nice    %sys %iowait   %idle
           0.60    0.00    2.40   18.16   78.84
Device:            tps   Blk_read/s   Blk_wrtn/s   Blk_read   Blk_wrtn
cciss/c0d0       27.94         0.00      1173.65          0       5880
```

As you can see, the load is 1.25 and IOWait is peaking at 20% - this is not good. If your IO wait is low but your MySQL is taking +%50 CPU this is also not good. Check your MySQL install for the following variables:

```
mysql> show variables;
| innodb_additional_mem_pool_size | 1048576     |
| innodb_autoextend_increment     | 8           |
| innodb_buffer_pool_awe_mem_mb   | 0           |
| innodb_buffer_pool_size         | 8388608     |
```

PacketFence relies heavily on InnoDB, so you should increase the `buffer_pool` size from the default values.

Shutdown PacketFence and MySQL

```
# /etc/init.d/packetfence stop
Shutting down PacketFence...
[...]
# /etc/init.d/mysql stop
Stopping MySQL:                                        [  OK  ]
```

Edit `/etc/my.cnf` (or your local `my.cnf`):

```
[mysqld]
# Set buffer pool size to 50-80% of your computer's memory
innodb_buffer_pool_size=800M
innodb_additional_mem_pool_size=20M
innodb_flush_log_at_trx_commit=2
innodb_file_per_table
# allow more connections
max_connections=700
# set cache size
key_buffer_size=900M
table_cache=300
query_cache_size=256M
# enable slow query log
log_slow_queries = ON
```

Start up MySQL and PacketFence

```
# /etc/init.d/mysqld start
Starting MySQL:                                            [  OK  ]
# /etc/init.d/packetfence start
Starting PacketFence...
[...]
```

Wait 10 minutes for PacketFence to initial the network map and re-check iostat and CPU

```
# uptime
12:01:58 up 235 days,  1:46,  1 user, load average: 0.15, 0.39, 0.52
# iostat 5
Device:            tps   Blk_read/s   Blk_wrtn/s   Blk_read   Blk_wrtn
cciss/c0d0        8.00         0.00        75.20          0        376

avg-cpu:  %user   %nice    %sys %iowait   %idle
           0.60    0.00    2.99   13.37   83.03

Device:            tps   Blk_read/s   Blk_wrtn/s   Blk_read   Blk_wrtn
cciss/c0d0       14.97         0.00       432.73          0       2168
avg-cpu:  %user   %nice    %sys %iowait   %idle
           0.20    0.00    2.60    6.60   90.60

Device:            tps   Blk_read/s   Blk_wrtn/s   Blk_read   Blk_wrtn
cciss/c0d0        4.80         0.00        48.00          0        240
```

## MySQL optimization tool

We recommend that you run the MySQL Tuner on your database setup after a couple of weeks to help you identify MySQL configuration improvement. The tool is bundled with PacketFence and can be run from the command-line:

```
# /usr/local/bin/pftest mysql
```

## Keeping tables small

Over time, some of the tables will grow large and this will drag down performance (this is especially true on a wireless setup).

One such table is the `locationlog` table. We recommend that closed entries in this table be moved to the archive table `locationlog_archive` after some time. A closed record is one where the `end_time` field is set to a date (strictly speaking it is when `end_time` is not null and not equals to 0).

We provide a script called `database-backup-and-maintenance.sh` located in `addons/` that performs this cleanup in addition to optimize tables on Sunday and daily backups.

## Avoid "Too many connections" problems

In a wireless context, there tends to be a lot of connections made to the database by our `freeradius` module. The default MySQL value tend to be low (100) so we encourage you to increase that value to at least 300. See http://dev.mysql.com/doc/refman/5.0/en/too-many-connections.html for details.

## Avoid "Host <hostname> is blocked" problems

In a wireless context, there tend to be a lot of connections made to the database by our freeradius module. When the server is loaded, these connection attempts can timeout. If a connection times out during connection, MySQL will consider this a connection error and after 10 of these (by default) he will lock the host out with a:

```
Host 'host_name' is blocked because of many connection errors. Unblock with
 'mysqladmin flush-hosts'
```

This will grind PacketFence to a halt so you want to avoid that at all cost. One way to do so is to increase the number of maximum connections (see above), to periodically flush hosts or to allow more connection errors. See http://dev.mysql.com/doc/refman/5.0/en/blocked-host.html for details.

## Using Percona XtraBackup

When dealing with a large database, the database backup and maintenance script (`/usr/local/pf/addons/database-backup-and-maintenance.sh`) which uses mysqldump may create a long lock on your database which may cause service to hang.

This is fixed easily by using Percona XtraBackup which can complete a full database backup without locking your tables.

The installation instructions below are made for CentOS 6 but adjusting them to CentOS 7 or Debian should only be a matter of installing the proper packages for your MySQL/MariaDB version.

First install the Percona repository:

```
# yum install http://www.percona.com/downloads/percona-release/redhat/0.1-3/
percona-release-0.1-3.noarch.rpm
```

Make sure to disable the newly installed repository not to interfere with future updates:

```
# sed -i -e 's/^enabled\ \=.*/enabled = 0/g' /etc/yum.repos.d/percona-
release.repo
```

Next, install Percona XtraBackup by manually specifying the Percona repository:

```
# yum install percona-xtrabackup-20 --enablerepo=percona-release-`uname -m`
```

Note

A more recent version of Percona XtraBackup can be used but only if you are running a recent version of MySQL.

Once this is done, grant the proper rights to the **pf** user (or the one you configured in pf.conf):

```
# mysql -u root -p
mysql> GRANT RELOAD, LOCK TABLES, REPLICATION CLIENT ON *.* TO 'pf'@'localhost';
mysql> FLUSH PRIVILEGES;
```

Next, run the maintenance script `/usr/local/pf/addons/database-backup-and-maintenance.sh` and ensure that the following line is part of the output:

```
innobackupex: completed OK!
```

If the backup fails, check `/usr/local/pf/logs/innobackup.log` for details and refer to the Percona XtraBackup documentation for troubleshooting.

Note

In the event that you want to stop using Percona XtraBackups for your MySQL backups, simply uninstall it and the database script will fallback to mysqldump.

# Captive Portal Optimizations

## Avoid captive portal overload due to non-browser HTTP requests

By default we allow every query to be redirected and reach PacketFence for the captive portal operation. In a lot of cases, this means that a lot of non-user initiated queries reach PacketFence and waste its resources for nothing since they are not from browsers. (iTunes, Windows update, MSN Messenger, Google Desktop, ...).

Since version 4.3 of PacketFence, you can define HTTP filters for Apache from the configuration of PacketFence.

Some rules have been enabled by default, like one to reject requests with no defined user agent. All rules, including some examples, are defined in the configuration file apache_filters.conf.

Filters are defined with at least two blocks. First are the tests. For example:

```
[get_ua_is_dalvik]
filter = user_agent
method = GET
operator = match
value = Dalvik
```

```
[get_uri_not_generate204]
filter = uri
method = GET
operator = match_not
value = /generate_204
```

The last block defines the relationship between the tests and the desired action. For example:

```
[block_dalvik:get_ua_is_dalvik&get_uri_not_generate204]
action = 501
redirect_url =
```

This filter will return an error code (501) if the user agent is Dalvik and the URI doesn't contain _/generate_204.

# Dashboard Optimizations (statistics collection)

The collection and aggregation of statistics in the whisper database can be I/O intensive per moment. This means that it can be beneficial to separate them on another disk even if it is a virtual disk that will share the same underlying physical disk.

First, add a disk in your virtual machine or bare metal server and reboot (this example will use /dev/sdb as the new device.

Make sure packetfence is stopped:

```
# service packetfence stop
```

Create an ext4 partition:

```
# mkfs.ext4 /dev/sdb
```

Then move the old databases to a backup point:

```
# mv /usr/local/pf/var/graphite /usr/local/pf/var/graphite.bak
```

Mount your new disk and check that it is mounted:

```
# echo "/dev/sdb /usr/local/pf/var/graphite          ext4    defaults        1
 1" >> /etc/fstab
# mkdir /usr/local/pf/var/graphite
# mount -a
# dh -h
```

Apply the proper user rights and restore your database from your backup

```
# chown pf.pf /usr/local/pf/var/graphite
# cp -frp /usr/local/pf/var/graphite.bak/* /usr/local/pf/var/graphite/
```

Start packetfence and make sure your stats are still there and being collected properly. Then remove the backup you made `rm -fr /usr/local/pf/var/graphite.bak/`.

# Troubleshooting

This section will address specific problems and known solutions.

## "Internet Explorer cannot display the webpage"

Problem: Internet Explorer 8-10 may raise an "Internet Explorer cannot display the webpage" error while attempting to access PacketFence administration interface because TLSv1.2 is not activated but required since PacketFence 7.

Solution:

- PacketFence administration interface is not started:

  ```
  # cd /usr/local/pf
  # bin/pfcmd service httpd.admin start
  ```

- It is strongly advised that you update your browser to Internet Explorer 11 or download an alternative.
- TLSv1.2 needs to be activated manually in Internet Explorer 8-10.

  ```
  Within Internet Explorer: click Tools, Internet Options, Advanced and make sure
   that TLS v1.2 is enabled under the security section. Retry.
  ```

Chapter 23

# Additional Information

For more information, please consult the mailing archives or post your questions to it. For details, see:

- packetfence-announce@lists.sourceforge.net: Public announcements (new releases, security warnings etc.) regarding PacketFence
- packetfence-devel@lists.sourceforge.net: Discussion of PacketFence development
- packetfence-users@lists.sourceforge.net: User and usage discussions

Chapter 24

# Commercial Support and Contact Information

For any questions or comments, do not hesitate to contact us by writing an email to: support@inverse.ca.

Inverse (http://inverse.ca) offers professional services around PacketFence to help organizations deploy the solution, customize, migrate versions or from another system, performance tuning or aligning with best practices.

Hourly rates or support packages are offered to best suit your needs.

Please visit http://inverse.ca/ for details.

Chapter 25

# GNU Free Documentation License

Please refer to http://www.gnu.org/licenses/fdl-1.2.txt for the full license.

# Appendix A. Administration Tools

## pfcmd

`pfcmd` is the command line interface to most PacketFence functionalities.

When executed without any arguments **`pfcmd`** returns a basic help message with all main options:

```
Usage:
  pfcmd <command> [options]

   Commands
    cache                       | manage the cache subsystem
    checkup                     | perform a sanity checkup and report any
 problems
    class                       | view violation classes
    configreload                | reload the configution
    fingerbank                  | Fingerbank related commands
    floatingnetworkdeviceconfig | query/modify floating network devices
 configuration parameters
    help                        | show help for pfcmd commands
    ifoctetshistorymac          | accounting history
    ifoctetshistoryswitch       | accounting history
    ifoctetshistoryuser         | accounting history
    import                      | bulk import of information into the database
    ipmachistory                | IP/MAC history
    locationhistorymac          | Switch/Port history
    locationhistoryswitch       | Switch/Port history
    networkconfig               | query/modify network configuration parameters
    node                        | manipulate node entries
    pfconfig                    | interact with pfconfig
    connectionprofileconfig     | query/modify connection profile configuration
 parameters
    reload                      | rebuild fingerprint or violations tables
 without restart
    service                     | start/stop/restart and get PF daemon status
    schedule                    | Nessus scan scheduling
    switchconfig                | query/modify switches.conf configuration
 parameters
    version                     | output version information
    violationconfig             | query/modify violations.conf configuration
 parameters

  Please view "pfcmd help <command>" for details on each option
```

The node view option shows all information contained in the node database table for a specified MAC address

```
# /usr/local/pf/bin/pfcmd node view 52:54:00:12:35:02
mac|pid|detect_date|regdate|unregdate|lastskip|status|user_agent|computername|
notes|last_arp|last_dhcp|switch|port|vlan|dhcp_fingerprint
52:54:00:12:35:02|1|2008-10-23 17:32:16||||unreg||||2008-10-23 21:12:21|||||
```

# Appendix B. Restoring a Percona XtraBackup dump

If you enabled Percona XtraBackup for your nightly backup, you can use the following instructions to restore it. In this example we will be restoring `/root/backup/packetfence-db-dump-innobackup-2016-12-20_00h31.xbstream.gz`

First, create a restore directory, move the backup to it and gunzip the backup:

```
# mkdir /root/backup/restore
# cd /root/backup/restore
# cp ../packetfence-db-dump-innobackup-2016-12-20_00h31.xbstream.gz .
# gunzip packetfence-db-dump-innobackup-2016-12-20_00h31.xbstream.gz
```

Then extract the xbstream data:

```
# xbstream -x < packetfence-db-dump-innobackup-2016-12-20_00h31.xbstream
```

Once done, you should have a lot of files that were extracted in the restore dir. Now, lets place the xbstream back in the backup directory

```
# mv packetfence-db-dump-innobackup-2016-12-20_00h31.xbstream ../
```

Next, install qpress (available from the percona repository) and process any qp file that were extracted:

CentOS:

```
# yum install qpress --enablerepo=percona-release-`uname -m`
```

Debian:

```
# apt-key adv --keyserver keys.gnupg.net --recv-keys 1C4CBDCDCD2EFD2A
# echo 'deb http://repo.percona.com/apt VERSION main' >> /etc/apt/sources.list
# echo 'deb-src http://repo.percona.com/apt VERSION main' >> /etc/apt/
sources.list
# apt-get update
# apt-get install qpress
```

```
# for i in $(find -name "*.qp"); do qpress -vd $i $(dirname ${i}) && rm -f $i;
 done
```

Next, apply the innodb log:

```
# innobackupex --apply-log ./
```

We will now stop MySQL, move the existing data directory and replace it by the data that was extracted:

## Note

On Debian the service will be called **`mysql`** and on CentOS 7 **`mariadb`**. Make sure you adjust the commands above to your environment.

```
# service mysqld stop
# mv /var/lib/mysql /var/lib/mysql.bak
# mkdir /var/lib/mysql
# mv * /var/lib/mysql
# chown -R mysql: /var/lib/mysql
# service mysqld start
```

Should the service fail to start, make sure you look into the MySQL error logs.

www.ingramcontent.com/pod-product-compliance
Lightning Source LLC
LaVergne TN
LVHW060142070326
832902LV00018B/2917
* 9 7 8 9 8 8 8 4 0 7 1 8 7 *